Speak the truth to the people
Talk sense to the people
Free them with reason
Free them with honesty
Free the people with Love and Courage and Care for their Being

—Marie Evans

SPEAKING THE TRUTH

Ecumenism, Liberation, and Black Theology

by

JAMES H. CONE

William B. Eerdmans Publishing Company
Grand Rapids, Michigan

To William E. Hordern
and
Lester B. Scherer

9-86

Library of Congress Cataloging-in-Publication Data

Cone, James H.
  Speaking the truth.

  1. Black theology. 2. Liberation theology.
3. Ecumenical movement. I. Title.
BT82.7.C68 1986   230'.08996073   86-16627

ISBN 0-8028-0226-5

Contents

Acknowledgments

MANY PEOPLE READ MY MANUSCRIPT AND OFFERED HELPFUL COM-
ments. They include Lester Scherer, Kelly Brown, Lydia
Hernandez, Gerald Shepard, Dwight Hopkins, Ben Ramsey, and
Sherrill Holland.

I also must express my gratitude to the persons who invited me
to speak at universities, seminaries, colleges, community groups,
and churches in the United States, Europe, Africa, Asia, Latin
America, and the Caribbean. The dialogue with many persons in
various contexts has challenged me to think more deeply about
the meaning of the gospel in the struggle for human freedom.

A word of appreciation is due to President Donald Shriver and
Dean Milton McC. Gatch of Union Seminary for their support of
my research and writing.

PREACHING THE GOSPEL IS NOT EASY IN A CHURCH DEFINED BY THE denominational interests of status-seeking clergy and laypersons. Doing Christian theology is difficult in a seminary or university determined by the academic interests of privileged professors and students. Speaking the truth can be politically dangerous in a society defined according to the socio-economic interests of the rich. Preaching the gospel, doing Christian theology, and speaking the truth are interrelated, and neither can be correctly understood apart from the liberation struggles of the poor and marginalized.

There can be no comprehension of the gospel apart from God's solidarity with the liberation struggles of the poor, because the freedom of the victims on earth is the eschatological sign of God's intention to redeem the whole creation. That was why Jesus entered the synagogue, opened the book of the prophet Isaiah, and said:

> The Spirit of the Lord is upon me,
> because he has anointed me to preach good news to the poor.
> He has sent me to proclaim release to the captives
> and recovering of sight to the blind,
> to set at liberty those who are oppressed,
> to proclaim the acceptable year of the Lord.
>
> Luke 4:18-19, RSV

The church of Jesus Christ is that community that can read the signs of the time, seeing God's struggle in the struggle of the poor. As ambassadors of Jesus Christ, Christians have no choice but to join the movement of liberation on the side of the poor, fighting against the structures of injustice. Faith in Jesus Christ, therefore, is not only an affirmation that we utter in Sunday worship and at other church gatherings. Faith is a commitment, a deeply felt experience of being called by the Spirit of Christ to bear witness to God's coming liberation by fighting for the freedom of the poor *now*.

Theology is the critical side of faith. It exposes what passes for faith but is actually faith's opposite. Preaching spirited sermons, singing beautiful hymns of praise to God, praying fervent prayers, and testifying and shouting in God's name are not enough to assure faith's authenticity. Without a practical commitment to validate faith's claim, what we say about God, Jesus Christ, and the Holy Spirit becomes nothing but pious talk that makes persons feel good, similar to the excitement derived from musical and sporting events. Theology is the church applying a *critical* self-evaluation of what it says and does on behalf of the one who defines the church's identity—namely, Jesus Christ.

These essays represent my attempt to "speak the truth" to African-American Christians in particular and to all Christians generally. It is important for the reader to know that they were written during the ten-year period 1975-85 and were presented to various audiences—churches and community groups, seminaries and universities, conferences and theological societies. Some have been published in theological journals, encyclopedias, and edited collections, while others are published here for the first time.

I do not claim to have spoken the last word on these issues, but I do hope that I have said an important word about the gospel for the time and place in which the essays were written. I also hope that they will provide some helpful insights for those Christians throughout the world who are trying to speak the truth with love, courage, and care for the poor and voiceless people of the land.

PART I

Black Theology as Liberation Theology

FROM THE TIME OF SLAVERY, BLACK REFLECTIONS ON THE CHRISTIAN faith have emphasized the idea of liberation as the heart of the gospel of Jesus. In the five essays of this section, the theme of liberation is analyzed theologically with emphases on its contemporary manifestations in the struggle of African-Americans to achieve justice in the United States.

In the first essay, "Christian Theology and Scripture as the Expression of God's Liberating Activity for the Poor," I argue that the culture of the oppressed must be used as the primary source for explicating the meaning of the gospel for our time. As will be obvious to my black critics, I am also responding to their criticism that my version of black theology (especially in *Black Theology and Black Power* [Seabury, 1969] and *A Black Theology of Liberation* [Lippincott, 1970]) is not really *black*, because I have not used black history and culture as the primary source to define it. Black critics claimed that my theology was defined by white concepts and not the black experience. Like *The Spirituals and the Blues* (Seabury, 1972) and *God of the Oppressed* (Seabury, 1975), this essay serves as a corrective to a weakness of my initial perspective on black theology.

The debate about the sources of black theology is closely related to the discussion about the relationship between spiritual and political liberation. If the sources of black theology must be derived from oppressed African-Americans, then the central meaning of black liberation cannot be reduced to the historical deliverance of slaves from bondage. It must be more than that. The "more," as I attempt to describe it in "Sanctification and Liberation in the Black Religious Tradition," is black people's ability to live in history without being determined by its limitations. No event expresses this transcendent truth more clearly than Sunday worship in the black church.

As there is a danger in overemphasizing politics in black theology, so there is a danger in placing too much stress on spirituality. Black spirituality can be misused and distorted. "Christian Faith and Political Praxis" represents my attempt to articulate an appropriate balance between faith and politics, between the worship of God in church and the liberation of persons from injustice in society. Unless Christians work out the proper balance between faith and social practice, they will inevitably fall victim to Marx's challenging critique of religion as the opium of the people.

Recently, a significant minority in the American Catholic Church has made a creative balance between faith and politics. In opposition to the Catholic ecclesiastical and American political establishments, they have expressed their solidarity with the struggles for justice among the poor in Latin America. But like many white Protestants, Catholics have not been sufficiently self-critical of their theological claims about freedom and justice, especially in relation to African-Americans. "A Theological Challenge to the American Catholic Church" was written at the request of the organizers of the conference on "Voices for Justice," held at the College of Notre Dame (Baltimore, July 1983). I hesitated when asked to give a critical evaluation of the American Catholic Church's view of justice as seen from the perspective of a black Protestant liberation theologian. I was acutely aware of my lack of personal knowledge regarding the theology and practice of the Catholic Church, and I expressed this concern to black and white Catholics. But both groups insisted that I speak frankly about the gospel and justice when viewed in the light of the Catholic Church's treatment of its black members.

Nothing has challenged the role of the Christian faith in the struggle of the poor for liberation more than the problem of violence. If God is the liberator of the oppressed from unjust suffering, does that mean that violence is an acceptable means for achieving justice? The relationship between the Christian faith and violence is a much-debated issue in the history of Christian theology. The last essay in Part I, "Violence and Vengeance: A Perspective," was presented as a "discussion starter" at a conference and not intended as an academic analysis of the theme. I merely wanted to stress the complexity of the theme and the need for Christians to express their solidarity with the victims of violence.

Christian Theology and Scripture as the Expression of God's Liberating Activity for the Poor

THEOLOGY IS LANGUAGE ABOUT GOD. *CHRISTIAN* THEOLOGY IS language about God's liberating activity in the world on behalf of the freedom of the oppressed. Any talk about God that fails to make God's liberation of the oppressed its starting point is not Christian. It may be philosophical and have some relation to Scripture, but it is not Christian. For the word "Christian" connects theology inseparably to God's will to set the captives free.

I realize that this understanding of theology and Christianity is not the central view of the Western theological tradition and neither is it the dominant viewpoint of contemporary Euro-American theology. However, truth ought not to be defined by the majority or by the dominant intellectual interest of university academicians. The purpose of this essay is to examine the theological presuppositions that underlie the claim that Christian theology is language about God's liberation of the victim from social and political oppression.

I

My contention that Christian theology is language about God's liberating activity for the poor is based upon the assumption that Scripture is the primary source of theological speech. To use Scripture as the starting point of theology does not rule out other sources, such as philosophy, tradition, and our contemporary context. It simply means that Scripture will define how these sources will function in theology.

This essay originally was presented at the annual meeting of the Society for the Study of Black Religion (1975) and later appeared as "What Is Christian Theology?" in *Encounter* 43 (Spring 1982): 117-28.

That Christian theology must begin with Scripture appears self-evident. Without this basic witness Christianity would be meaningless. This point seems so obvious to me that it is almost impossible to think otherwise. However, the point does need clarification. There are many perspectives on Scripture. There are some who regard it as infallible, and there are others who say that it is simply an important body of literature. There are nearly as many perspectives on Scripture as there are theologians. While I cannot assess the validity of the major viewpoints, I can state what I believe to be the central message of Scripture.

I believe that my perspective on Scripture is derived from Scripture itself. Since others, with different perspectives, would say the same thing, I can only explain the essential structure of my hermeneutical perspective. It seems clear to me that whatever else we may say about Scripture, it is first and foremost a story of Israelite people who believed that Yahweh was involved in their history. In the Old Testament, the story begins with the first Exodus of Hebrew slaves from Egypt and continues through the second Exodus from Babylon and the rebuilding of the Temple. To be sure, there are many ways to look at this story, but the import of the biblical message is clear on this point: God's salvation is revealed in the liberation of slaves from socio-political bondage. Indeed, God's judgment is inflicted on the people of Israel when they humiliate the poor and the orphans. "You shall not ill-treat any widow or fatherless child. If you do, be sure that I will listen if they appeal to me; my anger will be roused and I will kill you with the sword" (Exodus 22:23-24, NEB). Of course, there are other themes in the Old Testament, and they are important. But their importance is found in their illumination of the central theme of divine liberation. To fail to see this point is to misunderstand the Old Testament and thus to distort its message.

My contention that Scripture is the story of God's liberation of the poor also applies to the New Testament, where the story is carried to universal dimensions. The New Testament does not invalidate the Old. The meaning of Jesus Christ is found in God's will to make liberation not simply the property of one people but of all humankind. God became a poor Jew in Jesus and thus identified with the helpless in Israel. The cross of Jesus is nothing but God's will to be with and like the poor. The resurrection

means that God achieved victory over oppression, so that the
poor no longer have to be determined by their poverty. This is
true not only for the "house of Israel" but for all the wretched of
the land. The Incarnation, then, is simply God taking upon the
divine self human suffering and humiliation. The resurrection is
the divine victory over suffering, the bestowal of freedom to all
who are weak and helpless. This and nothing else is the central
meaning of the biblical story.

If theology is derived from this divine story, then it *must* be a
language about liberation. Anything else would be an ideological
distortion of the gospel message.

II

Because Christian theology begins and ends with the biblical story
of God's liberation of the weak, it is also christological language.
On this point Karl Barth was right. Unfortunately Barth did not
explicate this christological point with sufficient clarity, because
his theology was determined too much by the theological tradition of Augustine and Calvin and too little by Scripture. While
Barth's christological starting point enabled him to move closer to
the biblical message than most of his contemporaries, his understanding of theology was not derived from the biblical view of
Jesus Christ as the Liberator of the oppressed. Because Jesus the
Liberator is not central in Barth's christology, his view of theology
is also defective at this point.

Because theology begins with Scripture, it must also begin with
Christ. Christian theology is language about the crucified and
risen Christ who grants freedom to all who are falsely condemned
in an oppressive society. What else can the crucifixion mean except that God, the Holy One of Israel, became identified with the
victims of oppression? What else can the resurrection mean except that God's victory in Christ is the poor person's victory over
poverty? If theology does not take this seriously, how can it be
worthy of the name Christian? If the church, the community out
of which theology arises, does not make God's liberation of the
oppressed central in its mission and proclamation, how can it rest
easy with a condemned criminal as the dominant symbol of its
message?

III

Because Christian theology is more than the retelling of the biblical story, it also must do more than exegete Scripture. The meaning of Scripture is not self-evident in every situation. Therefore, it is theology's task to relate the message of the Bible to every situation. This is not an easy task, since situations are different, and God's word to humanity is not always self-evident.

Because theology must relate the message to the situation of the church's involvement in the world, theology must use other sources in addition to Scripture. On this point, Bultmann and Tillich are more useful than Barth, although they misrepresent the function of culture in theology. Unlike Barth, my disagreement with Bultmann and Tillich is not on whether theology should use culture (e.g., philosophy, sociology, and psychology) in the interpretation of the gospel. That our language about God is inseparably bound with our own historicity seems so obvious that to deny it is to become enslaved to our own ideology. Karl Barth notwithstanding, the natural theology issue is dead, at least to the extent that our language is never simply about God and nothing else however much we might wish it otherwise. This means that theology cannot avoid philosophy, sociology, and other perspectives on the world.

The issue, then, is not whether we can or ought to avoid speaking of human culture in the doing of theology. Rather the question is whether divine revelation in Scripture grants us a possibility of saying something about *God* that is *not* simply about ourselves. Unless this possibility is given, however small it might be, then there seems to be no point in talking about the distinction between white and black theology or the difference between falsehood and truth.

I believe that by focusing on Scripture, theology is granted the freedom to take seriously its social and political situation without being determined by it. Thus the question is not whether we take seriously our social existence but *how* and in *what* way we take it seriously. Whose social situation does our theology represent? For whom do we speak? The importance of Scripture in our theology is that it can help us to answer that question so as to represent the political interest of the One about whom Christianity speaks. By using Scripture, we are forced by Scripture itself to focus on our social existence, but not merely in terms of our own interests, though they are always involved. Scripture can liberate theology to be Christian in the contemporary situation. It can break the theologians out of their social ideologies and enable them to hear a word that is other than their own consciousness.

This "other" in theology is distinct but never separated from our social existence. God became human in Christ so that we are free to speak about God in terms of humanity. Indeed, any other talk is not about the crucified and risen Lord. The presence of the crucified and risen Christ as witnessed in Scripture determines whose social interest we must represent if we are to be faithful to him.

In an attempt to do theology in the light of this scriptural witness to the crucified and risen Christ as he is found in our contemporary situation, I have spoken of Christian theology as black theology. Of course there are other ways of talking about God which are also Christian. I have never denied that, and do not wish to deny it today. Christian theology can be written from the perspective of red, brown, and yellow peoples. It can also be written in the light of women's experience. In Japan, I have been impressed by the way that Korean Christians are hearing the word of divine liberation in an impressive Japanese culture. Christian theology can also be written from the perspective of class, as has been profoundly disclosed in the writings of Latin American liberation theologians. It is also possible to combine the issues of class, sex, and color, as was demonstrated in Letty Russell's *Human Liberation in a Feminist Perspective*. The possibilities are many and varied. There is not one Christian theology, but many Christian theologies which are valid expressions of the gospel of Jesus.

But it is not possible to do Christian theology apart from the biblical claim that God came in Christ to set the captives free. It is not possible to do Christian theology as if the poor do not exist. Indeed, there can be no Christian speech about God which does not represent the interest of the victims in our society. If we can just make that point an embodiment of our Christian identity, then we will have moved a long way since the days of Constantine.

IV

Because Christian theology is language about God's liberation of the weak as defined by Scripture in relation to our contemporary situation, Christian theology is inseparably connected with an oppressed community. If God is the God of the poor who is liberating them from bondage, how can we speak correctly about this God unless our language arises out of the community where God's presence is found? If Christian theology is language about the crucified and risen One, the One who has elected all for freedom, what else can it be than the language of those who are fighting for freedom?

My limitation of Christian theology to the oppressed community does not mean that everything the oppressed say about God is right because they are weak and helpless. To do that would be to equate the word of the oppressed with God's word. There is nothing in Scripture which grants this possibility. When the oppressed are inclined to use their position as a privilege, as an immunity from error, they do well to remember the scriptural witness to God's righteousness as other than anything human. On this point, Karl Barth was right: there is an infinite qualitative distinction between God and humanity.

When I limit Christian theology to the oppressed community, I intend to say nothing other than what I believe to be the central message of Scripture: God has chosen to disclose divine righteousness in the liberation of the poor. Therefore to be outside this community is to be in a place where one is excluded from the possibility of hearing and obeying God's word of liberation. By becoming poor and entrusting divine revelation to a carpenter from Nazareth, God makes clear where one has to be in order to hear the divine word and experience divine presence. If Jesus had been born in the king's court and had been an advisor to the emperor of Rome, then what I am saying would have no validity. If Jesus had made no distinction between the rich and the poor, the weak and the strong, then the Christian gospel would not be a word of liberation to the oppressed. If Jesus had not been crucified as a criminal of Rome and condemned as a blasphemer by the Jewish religious leaders, then my claim about Christian theology and the oppressed would be meaningless. It is because Scripture is so decisively clear on this issue that I insist that theology cannot separate itself from the cultural history of the oppressed if it intends to be faithful to the One who makes Christian language possible.

What then are we to say about these other so-called Christian theologies? To the extent that they fail to remain faithful to the central message of the gospel, they are heretical. In saying this, I do not intend to suggest that I have the whole truth and nothing but the truth. In fact I could be the heretic. Furthermore, I do not believe that the purpose of identifying heresy is to be able to distinguish the "good" people from the "bad" or infallible truth from error. I merely intend to say what I believe to be faithful to the gospel of Jesus as witnessed in Scripture—nothing more and nothing less. If we do not say what we believe, in love and faith and the hope that we are speaking and doing the truth, then why speak at all? If there is no distinction between truth and error, the gospel and heresy, then there is no way to say what Christian theology is. We must be able to say when language is not Christian—if not always, then at least sometimes.

I say that white North American theology is heresy not because I want to burn anybody at the stake. Far too many of my people have been lynched for me to suggest such nonsense. The identification of heresy is not for the purpose of making ultimate decisions about who shall live or die and who will be saved or damned. To know what heresy is, is to know what appears to be truth but is actually untruth. Thus it is for the sake of the truth of the gospel that we must say what truth is not.

The saying of what truth is, is intimately connected with the doing of truth. To know the truth is to do the truth. Speaking and doing are bound together so that what we say can be authenticated only by what we do. Unfortunately, the Western church has not always been clear on this point. Its mistake has often been the identification of heresy with word rather than action. By failing to explicate the connection between word and action, the church tended to identify the gospel with right speech and thus became the chief heretic. The church became so preoccupied with its own spoken word about God that it failed to hear and thus live according to God's word of freedom for the poor. From Augustine to Schleiermacher, it is hard to find a theologian in the Western church who defines the gospel in terms of God's liberation of the oppressed.

The same is true in much of the contemporary speech about God. It can be seen in the separation of theology from ethics and the absence of liberation in both. The chief mistake of contemporary white theology is not simply found in what it says about God, though that is not excluded. It is found in its separation of theory from praxis, and the absence of liberation in its analysis of the gospel.

V

The limitation of Christian theology to the oppressed community not only helps us to identify heresy, it also helps us to reexamine the sources of theological speech. The language of liberation must reflect the experiences of the people about whom we claim to speak. To say that one's speech is a theology of liberation does not in itself mean that it represents the oppressed. There are many theologies of liberation, not all of which represent the weak and the helpless. The difference between liberation theology in general and liberation theology in the Christian perspective is found in whether the language about freedom is derived from one's participation in the oppressed people's struggle. If one's language about freedom is derived from one's involvement in an oppressed people's struggle for freedom, then it is Christian language. It is a language that is accountable to the God encountered in the oppressed community, and not some abstract God in a theological textbook. To say that one's theology represents the poor means that the representation reflects the words and deeds of the poor. The theologian begins to talk like the poor, to pray like the poor, and to preach with the poor in mind. Instead of making Barth, Tillich, and Pannenberg the exclusive sources for the doing of theology, the true liberation theologian is compelled to hear the cries and the moans of the people who sing "I wish I knew how it would feel to be free, I wish I could break all the chains holdin' me."

What would theology look like if we were to take seriously the claim that Christian theology is poor people's speech about their hopes and dreams that one day "trouble will be no more"? One thing is certain: it would not look like most of the papers presented in the American Academy of Religion and the American Theological Society. Neither would it look like "process theology," "liberal theology," "Death of God theology," or a host of other adjectives academicians use to describe their intellectual endeavors.

Theology derived from the moans and shouts of oppressed black people defines a different set of problems than those found in the white theological textbooks. Instead of asking whether the Bible is infallible, black people want to know whether it is real— that is, whether the God to which it bears witness is present in their struggle. Black theology seeks to investigate the meaning of black people's confidence in the biblical claim that Jesus is the

way, the truth, and the life. Black theology is the consciousness of
the people analyzing the meaning of their faith when they have to
live in an extreme situation of suffering. How can black theology
remain faithful to the people and the God revealed in their struggle if it does not respect the people's conceptualizations of their
claim that "God will make a way of no way"? They really believe
that

> When you are troubled, burdened with care,
> And know not what to do;
> Fear ye not to call His Name
> And He will fix it for you.

Theology derived from the black experience must reflect the
rhythm and the mood, the passion and ecstasy, the joy and the
sorrow of a people in a struggle to free themselves from the
shackles of oppression. This theology must be black because the
people are black. It must deal with liberation because the people
are oppressed. It must be biblical because the people claim that
the God of the Exodus and the prophets and of Jesus and the
apostle Paul is involved in their history, liberating them from
bondage. A theology derived from black sources would have to
focus on Jesus Christ as the beginning and the end of faith, because this affirmation is a summary of the black testimony that
"Jesus picked me up, turned me round, left my feet on solid
ground." He is sometimes called the "Wheel in the middle of the
Wheel," the "Rose of Sharon," and the "Lord of Life." Black
people claim that he healed the sick, gave sight to the blind and
enabled the lame to walk. "Jesus," they say, "do most anything."

VI

The presence of Jesus as the starting point of black theology does
not mean that it can overlook the experience of suffering in black
life.[1] Any theology that takes liberation seriously must also take
seriously the continued presence of suffering in black life. How

1. For a further discussion of the theme of suffering in black religion, see
chap. 6, "God and Black Suffering," in my book *The Spirituals and the Blues* (New
York: Seabury Press, 1972) and chap. 8, "Divine Liberation and Black Suffering,"
in *God of the Oppressed* (New York: Seabury Press, 1975). This theme has been
much discussed by other black writers also; see especially William Jones, *Is God a
White Racist?* (New York: Doubleday, 1973).

can we claim that "God will fix it" for the poor when the poor still exist in poverty? The blues, folklore, and other secular expressions are constant reminders that a simplistic view of divine liberation is never adequate for a people in struggle against oppression. Black religion has never been silent on the theme of suffering. Indeed, black faith arose out of black people's experience of suffering. Without the brokenness of black existence, its pain and sorrow, there would be no reason for the existence of black faith.

> Nobody knows the trouble I've seen,
> Nobody knows my sorrow,
> Nobody knows the trouble I've seen,
> Glory, Hallelujah!

The "Glory, Hallelujah" at the end of that spiritual was not a denial of trouble but a faith affirmation that trouble does not have the last word on black existence. It means that evil and suffering, while still unquestionably present, cannot count decisively against black people's faith that Jesus is also present with them, fighting against trouble. His divine presence counts more than the pain that the people experience in their history. Jesus is the people's "rock in a weary land" and their "shelter in a time of storm." No matter how difficult the pains of life might become, they cannot destroy the people's confidence that victory over suffering has already been won in Jesus' resurrection. Thus the people sang:

> Sometimes I hangs my head an' cries,
> But Jesus going to wipe my weep'n eyes.

Of course, there is no evidence that black people's faith-claim is "objectively" or "scientifically" true. Thus when William Jones, a black critic of black theology, asks about the decisive liberation event in black history, he is asking the question from a vantage point that is external to black faith.[2] For black faith claims that Jesus is the only evidence one needs to have in order to be assured that God has not left the little ones alone in bondage. For those who stand outside of this faith, such a claim is a scandal—that is, foolishness to those whose wisdom is derived from European

2. See his *Is God a White Racist?* For a fuller critique of Jones, see chap. 8 of my *God of the Oppressed.*

intellectual history. "But to those who are called, . . . Christ [is] the power of God, and the wisdom of God" (1 Cor. 1:24). In black religion, Christ is the Alpha and Omega, the One who has come to make the first last and the last first. The knowledge of this truth is not found in philosophy, sociology, or psychology. It is found in the immediate presence of Jesus with the people, "buildin' them up where they are torn down and proppin' them up on every leanin' side." The evidence that Jesus is liberating them from bondage is found in their walking and talking with him, telling him all about their troubles. It is found in the courage and strength he bestows on the people as they struggle to humanize their environment.

These answers will not satisfy the problem of theodicy as defined by Sartre and Camus. But black faith assertions were never intended to be answers for the intellectual problems arising out of the European experience. They are *black* reflections on life and were intended as testimonies for the oppressed so that they would not give up in despair. They are not rational arguments. The truth of the claims is not found in whether the black faith perspective answers the theodicy problem as posed in Camus's *Plague* or Sartre's *Being and Nothingness*.[3] The truth of the black faith-claim is found in whether the people receive that extra strength to fight until freedom comes. Its truth is found in whether the people who are the victims of *white* philosophy and theology are led to struggle to realize the freedom they talk about. The same is true for a black theology or philosophy that seeks to speak on behalf of the people. Whether William Jones is right or whether my analysis is correct should not be decided on theoretical criteria derived from Western theology and philosophy. Pure theory is for those who have the leisure for reflection but not for the victims of the land. The truth, therefore, of our theological analysis ought to be decided by the historical *function* of our assertions in the community we claim to represent.

Whose analysis, Cone's or Jones's, leads to the historical praxis against oppression? I would contend that black humanism, as

3. William Jones refers to Camus and Sartre and their formulation of the problem of evil. I think that is a mistake, because the problem can easily become an intellectual issue for seminar discussions rather than something to which we are called to *fight* against in this world. I find nothing in Jones's formulation of the problem of evil that would lead me to fight against it in this world.

derived from Camus and Sartre, does not lead the people to the fight against oppression but rather to give up in despair, the feeling that there is little I can do about white power. But my analysis of black faith, with Jesus as the "Captain of the Old Ship of Zion" can lead the people to believe that their fight is not in vain. That was why Martin Luther King, Jr., could move the people to fight for justice. He had a dream that was connected with Jesus. Without Jesus, the people would have remained passive, and content with humiliation and suffering. When I turn to Western philosophy's analysis of metaphysics and ontology, I do not know whether King was right, if rightness is defined by white rationality. But in the faith context of black religion, King was right, because people were led to act out the faith they talked about. If black theology is to be a theology of and for this black faith, it will not bother too much about the logical contradictions of its assertions when they are compared with white Western philosophy. William Jones's humanism notwithstanding, some black folk still believe that

> Without God I could no nothing;
> Without God my life would fail;
> Without God my life would be rugged,
> Just like a ship without a sail.

Note the absence of philosophical skepticism in the next verse.

> Without a doubt, He is my Savior,
> Yes, my strength along my way;
> Yes, in deep water, He is my anchor,
> And through faith he'll keep me all the way.

It is because black people feel secure in "leaning and depending on Jesus" that they often lift their voices in praise and adoration, singing: "Thank you Jesus, I thank you Lord. For you brought me a mighty long ways. You've been my doctor, you've been my lawyer, and you've been my friend. You've been my everything!" These people *actually* believe that with Jesus' presence, they cannot lose. Victory over suffering and oppression is certain. If not now, then in God's own "good time," "one day, it will all be over." We will "cross the river of Jordan" and "sit down with the Father and argue with the Son" and "tell them about the world we just come from." Thus black people's struggle of freedom is not in vain. This is what black people mean when they sing: "I'm so glad that trouble don't last always." Because trouble does not have the last word, we can fight *now* in order to realize in our present what we know to be coming in God's future.

Sanctification and Liberation in the Black Religious Tradition, with Special Reference to Black Worship

SINCE THE APPEARANCE OF BLACK THEOLOGY IN THE LATE 1960S, much has been said and written about the theme of liberation in black religion.[1] The names of Henry Highland Garnet, David Walker, Daniel Payne, and Henry McNeil Turner have been widely quoted in black theological circles, because they related the Christian gospel to the politics of black liberation. For the same reason, such spirituals as "Go Down Moses," "O Freedom," and "Steal Away" are often quoted in contemporary black theological discourse. Black theologians are concerned to show the liberating character of black Christianity in our struggle for social and political justice. But in our effort to show that the gospel is political, we black theologians have sometimes been in danger of reducing black religion to politics and black worship to a political

---

1. The earliest publication on black theology was my *Black Theology and Black Power* (New York: Seabury Press, 1969); see also my *Black Theology of Liberation* (Philadelphia: Lippincott, 1970); *The Spirituals and the Blues* (New York: Seabury Press, 1972); and *God of the Oppressed* (New York: Seabury Press, 1975). Other writers on the subject include J. Deotis Roberts, *Liberation and Reconciliation: A Black Theology* (Philadelphia: Westminster Press, 1971) and *A Black Political Theology* (Philadelphia: Westminster Press, 1974); Major Jones, *Black Awareness: A Theology of Hope* (Nashville: Abingdon Press, 1971); William Jones, *Is God a White Racist?* (Garden City, N.Y.: Doubleday, 1973); and Cecil Cone, *The Identity Crisis in Black Theology* (Nashville: AMEC, 1975). For a historical account of the development of black religion and black theology, see Gayraud S. Wilmore, *Black Religion and Black Radicalism* (Garden City, N.Y.: Doubleday, 1972).

This essay was originally prepared for the Sixth Oxford Institute on Methodist Theological Studies, Lincoln College, Oxford, England, 18-28 July 1977. It also appeared in *Sanctification and Liberation*, ed. Theodore Runyon (Nashville: Abingdon Press, 1981), pp. 174-92.

17

strategy session, thereby distorting the essence of black religion. This point is forcefully stated—in fact overstated—by Cecil Cone in *Identity Crisis in Black Theology.* In this essay, my concern is to examine the spiritual foundation of black worship as reflected in its components of preaching, singing, shouting, conversion, prayer, and testimony. Hopefully I will be able to clarify the connection between the experience of holiness in worship and the struggle for political justice in the larger society.

The Holy Spirit and Black Worship

Black worship is essentially a spiritual experience of the truth of black life. The experience is spiritual because the people encounter the presence of the divine Spirit in their midst. Black worship is truthful because the Spirit's presence authenticates their experience of freedom by empowering them with courage and strength to bear witness in their present existence, what they know is coming in God's own eschatological future.

> Have I got a witness?
> Certainly Lord!
> Have I got a witness?
> Certainly Lord!
> Certainly, certainly, certainly Lord.

This call and response is an essential element of the black worship style. Black worship is a community happening wherein the people experience the truth of their lives as lived together in the struggle of freedom and held together by God's Spirit. There is no understanding of black worship apart from the presence of the Spirit who descends upon the gathered community, lighting a spiritual fire in their hearts. The divine Spirit is not a metaphysical entity but rather the power of Jesus, who breaks into the lives of the people giving them a new song to sing as confirmation of God's presence with them in historical struggle. It is the presence of the divine Spirit that accounts for the intensity in which black people engage in worship. There is no understanding of black worship apart from the rhythm of the song and sermon, the passion of prayer and testimony, the ecstasy of the shout and conversion as the people project their humanity in the togetherness of the Spirit.

The black church congregation is an eschatological community that lives as if the end of time were already at hand. The difference between the earliest Christian community as an eschatological congregation and the black church community is this: the post-resurrection community expected a complete cosmic transformation in Jesus' immediate return because the end of time was at hand. The eschatological significance of the black community is found in the people believing that the Spirit of Jesus is coming to visit them in the worship service each time two or three are gathered in his name and to bestow upon them a new vision of their future humanity. This eschatological revolution is not so much a cosmic change as it is a change in the people's identity, wherein they are no longer named by the world but named by the Spirit of Jesus. Roberta Flack expresses the significance of this eschatological change in the people's identity in her singing of "I told Jesus it would be all right if he changed my name. He told me that the world will turn away from you, child, if I changed your name." This change in identity affects not only one's relationship with the world but also with one's immediate family. "He told me that your father and mother won't know you, child, if I changed your name." Because the reality of the Spirit's liberating and sanctifying presence is so overwhelming on the believer's identity, the believer can still say with assurance: "I told Jesus it would be all right if he changed my name."

The Holy Spirit's presence with the people is a liberating experience. Black people who have been humiliated and oppressed by the structures of white society six days of the week gather together each Sunday morning in order to experience another definition of their humanity. The transition from Saturday to Sunday is not just a chronological change from the seventh to the first day of the week. It is rather a rupture in time, a *kairos*-event which produces a radical transformation in the people's identity. The janitor becomes the chairperson of the Deacon Board; the maid becomes the president of Stewardess Board Number 1. Everybody becomes Mr. and Mrs. or Brother and Sister. The last becomes first, making a radical change in the perception of one's self and one's calling in the society. Every person becomes somebody, and one can see the people's recognition of their newfound identity by the way they walk and talk and "carry themselves." They walk with a rhythm of an assurance that they know where they are going, and they talk as if they know the truth about which they speak. It is this experience of being radically transformed by the power of the Spirit which defines the primary style of black worship. This transformation is found not only in the titles of Deacons, Stewardesses, Trustees, and Ushers, but also in the excitement of the entire congregation at worship. To be at the end of time where one has been given a new name requires a passionate response commensurate with the felt power of the Spirit in one's heart.

In the act of worship itself, the experience of liberation becomes a constituent of the community's being. In this context, liberation is not exclusively a political event but also an eschatological happening. It is the power of God's Spirit invading the lives of the people, "buildin' them up where they are torn down and proppin' them up on every leanin' side." When a song is sung right and the sermon is delivered in response to the Spirit, the people experience the eschatological presence of God in their midst. Liberation is no longer a future event, but a present happening in the worship itself. That is why it is hard to sit still in a black worship service. For the people claim that "if you don't put anything into the service, you sure won't get anything out of it." Black worship demands involvement. Sometimes a sister does not plan to participate too passionately, but before she knows what is happening "a little fire starts to burning and a little prayer-wheel starts to turning in her heart." In response to the Spirit and its liberating presence, she begins to move to the Spirit's power. How and when she moves depends upon the way the Spirit touches her soul and engages her in the dynamics of the community at worship. She may acknowledge the Spirit's presence with a song.

> Every time I feel the spirit
> Moving in my heart I will pray.
> Every time I feel the spirit
> Moving in my heart I will pray.
>
> Upon the mountain my Lord spoke.
> Out of His mouth came fire and smoke.
> In the valley on my knees,
> Asked my Lord, Have mercy, please.
>
> Every time I feel the spirit
> Moving in my heart I will pray . . .

However, song is only one possible response to the Spirit's presence. God's Spirit also may cause a person to preach, pray, or testify. "I believe I will testify for what the Lord has done for me" is an often-heard response in the black church. But more of the presence of the Spirit elicits what W. E. B. DuBois called the "Frenzy"[2] and what the people call the "shout," which refers not to sound but to bodily movement. "When the Lord gets ready," the people claim, "you've got to move"—that is, to "stand up and let the world know that you are not ashamed to be known as a child of God."

There is no authentic black worship service apart from the presence of the Spirit, God's power to be with and for the people. It is not unusual for the people to express their solidarity with John on the island of Patmos and to say with him: "I was in the Spirit on the Lord's day" (Rev. 1:10, KJV). Like John, black people believe that to be in the Spirit is to experience the power of another presence in their midst. The Spirit is God's guarantee that the little ones are never, no not ever, left alone in their struggle for freedom. God's Spirit is God's way of being with the people, enabling them to shout for joy when the people have no obvious reason in their lives to warrant happiness. The Spirit sometimes makes you run and clap your hands; at other times, you want just to sit still and perhaps pat your feet, wave your hands, and hum the melody of a song: "Ain't no harm to praise the Lord."

It is difficult for an outsider to understand what is going on in a black worship service. To know what is happening in this eschatological event, one cannot approach this experience as a detached observer in the role of a sociologist of religion or as a psychologist, looking for an explanation not found in the life-experiences of the people. One must come as a participant in black reality, willing to be transformed by one's encounter with the Spirit. If one is willing to let the Spirit have her way, being open to what God has in store for him, then he will probably understand what the people mean when they sing:

> Glory, glory, hallelujah
> Since I laid my burdens down.
> Glory, glory, hallelujah,
> Since I laid my burdens down.
>
> I'm going home to live with Jesus,
> Since I laid my burdens down.
> I'm going home to live with Jesus,
> Since I laid my burdens down.

2. See DuBois, *The Souls of Black Folk* (New York: Fawcett, 1968), pp. 141-42.

It is the people's response to the presence of the Spirit that creates the unique style of black worship. The style of black worship is a constituent of its content, and both elements point to the theme of liberation. Unlike whites, who often drive a wedge between content and style in worship (as in their secular-sacred distinction), blacks believe that a sermon's content is inseparable from the way in which it is proclaimed. Blacks are deeply concerned about *how* things are said in prayer and testimony and their effect upon those who hear them. The way I say "I love the Lord, he heard my cry" cannot be separated from my intended meaning as derived from my existential and historical setting. For example, if I am one who has just escaped from slavery, and my affirmation is motivated by that event, I will express my faith-claim with the passion and ecstasy of one who was once lost and now found. There will be no detachment in my proclamation of freedom. Only those who do not know bondage existentially can speak of liberation "objectively." Only those who have not been in the "valley of death" can sing the songs of Zion as if they are uninvolved. Black worship is derived from the meeting with the Lord in the struggle to be free. If one has not met the Spirit of God in the struggle for freedom, there can be no joy and no reason to sing with ecstatic passion "I am so glad that trouble don't last always."

The Components of Black Worship

There are six principal components of black worship: preaching, singing, shouting, conversion, prayer, and testimony.

Expressing his admiration for the black preacher, W. E. B. DuBois called him, among other things, "a leader, a politician, an orator, a 'boss,' an intriguer, an idealist."[3] DuBois, however, did not include "prophet" in his list—certainly the black preacher's most important office. The black preacher is primarily a prophet who speaks God's truth to the people. The sermon, therefore, is a prophetic oration wherein the preacher "tells it like it is" according to the divine Spirit who speaks through him or her.

In the black church, the sermon is not intended to be an intellectual discourse on things divine or human. That would make the preached Word a human word and thus dependent upon the

3. DuBois, *The Souls of Black Folk*, p. 141.

intellectual capacity of the preacher. In order to separate the preached Word from ordinary human discourse and thereby connect it with prophecy, the black church emphasizes the role of the Spirit in preaching. No one is an authentic preacher in the black church tradition until he or she is called by the Spirit. No person, according to this tradition, should decide to enter the ministry on his or her own volition. Preaching is not a human choice; it is a divine choice. Just as God called Amos from Tekoa, Jeremiah while he was only a youth, Isaiah in the temple, and Paul on the Damascus road, so also God speaks directly to those whom God sets aside for the ministry. It is expected that preachers will give an account of their calling, about how and when the Lord touched their soul and set them aside for the proclamation of divine truth. Some preachers testify that it was late one Wednesday evening or early one Thursday morning. There is no rigidity about the time or even how the call came. But what is important is the authenticity of the call so that the people know that they are encountering God's Word through the sermon's oration, and not simply the personal interest of a given preacher.

However, the question may be legitimately asked: "How do the people really *know* when the preacher is telling the truth about his or her calling?" There were false prophets in the Old Testament; there are also false preachers in the black community. But there are criteria derived from the community and the biblical witness for the detection of imposters. They include such things as more interest in salary and prestige than in the spiritual, social, and political welfare of the people. There are many spirits in the black community that have nothing to do with God's Holy Spirit. The people can usually detect which spirit is at work during the sermon's oration by the logical praxis which proceeds from the spoken word. They know when pastors and bishops are not telling God's truth but speaking for their own personal gain, and no amount of clever sermonic delivery can change that fact. When they benefit from what they say and consciously manipulate the congregation for financial gain, then we can be certain that the spirit they disclose is closer to Satan than to God. The prophet never gains personally from his proclamation of truth. He is sometimes ostracized by the people because of what he says. Speaking for God often lands a prophet in jail, as was true of Jeremiah in the seventh century before Christ and Martin Luther King, Jr., in the twentieth century after Christ, because God's righteousness demands justice for the poor and empowerment of the weak. In church politics where selfishness, greed, and pride define ministers' relationships with each other and laypeople, the prophet is one who stands before the church and all who silently tolerate it and says what Nathan said to David: "Thou art the man!" And any layperson, pastor, or bishop who fails to speak God's truth against the evil they know exists in the church is no different from Judas, who sold the Lord for thirty pieces of silver. Black preachers who act in this manner are defiling a great tradition.

In the black tradition, preaching as prophecy is essentially telling God's story. "Telling the story" is the essence of black preaching. It means proclaiming with appropriate rhythm and passion the connection between the Bible and the history of black people. What has Scripture to do with our life in white society and the struggle to be *somebody* in it? To answer that question, the preacher must be able to tell God's story so that the people will experience its liberating presence in their midst. That is why the people always ask of every preacher: "Can the Reverend tell the story?" To tell the story is to act out with the rhythm of one's voice and the movement of the body, the truth about which he or she speaks. We can say of the black preacher what B. D. Napier says about the Old Testament prophet: "The symbolic acts of the prophets are simply graphic, pictorial extensions of the Word, possessing both for the prophet and for his observers-hearers a quality of realism probably unfathomable psychologically to the Western mind."[4]

If the people do not say "Amen" or give some other passionate response, this usually means that the Spirit has chosen not to speak through the preacher at that time. The absence of the Spirit could mean that the preacher is dependent too much on his or her own capacity to speak or that the congregation was too involved in its own personal quarrels. Whatever the case, the absence of a "hallelujah" and "praise the Lord" when the preacher speaks God's Word is uncharacteristic of a black worship service. For these responses let preachers know that they are on the right track and that what they say rings true to the Spirit's presence in their midst. An "Amen" involves the people in the proclamation and commits them to the divine truth which they hear proclaimed. It means that the people recognize that what is said is

4. Napier, "Prophet, Prophetism," in *The Interpreter's Dictionary of the Bible*, vol. 3 (Nashville: Abingdon Press, 1962), p. 912.

not just Reverend So-and-so's idea but God's claim, which God lays upon the people.

Next to preaching, song is the most important ingredient in black worship. Most black people believe that the Spirit does not descend without a song. Song opens the hearts of the people for the coming of God's Spirit. That is why most church services are opened with a song and why most preachers would not attempt to preach without having the congregation sing a "special" song in order to prepare the people for God's Word. Song not only prepares the people for the Spirit but also intensifies the power of the Spirit's presence with the people. Through song a certain mood is created in the congregation, and the people can experience the quality of the Spirit's presence. One cannot force the Spirit to come through manipulation. The Spirit always remains free of human choice. By singing a song, the people know whether they have the proper disposition for the coming of the Spirit.

In many black congregations, there are special songs which are led by particular people, and no one would dare sing another person's song. That would be a sure way of "killing the Spirit." I grew up in Macedonia African Methodist Episcopal Church in Bearden, Arkansas, and I can remember several people's songs in that congregation. My mother's song was

> This little light of mine,
> I'm goin' to let it shine;
> This little light of mine,
> I'm goin' to let it shine,
> Let it shine, let it shine.

Sister Ora Wallace, unquestionably the best singer at Macedonia, would always sing:

> I'm workin' on the buildin'
> It's a true foundation,
> I'm holdin' up the blood-stained banner for my Lord.
> Just as soon as I get through,
> Through working on the buildin'
> I'm goin' up to heaven to get my reward.

Of all the favorite songs of Macedonia, I will never forget Sister Drew Chavis's song, because she sang it with such intensity and passion that it never failed to bring tears in the eyes of most people assembled.

> Precious Lord, take my hand,
> Lead me on, let me stand,
> I am tired, I am weak, I am worn.
> Through the storm, through the night
> Lead me on to the light,
> Take my hand, precious Lord,
> Lead me home.

By the time she reached the second stanza and began to sing "when my life is almost gone, Hear my cry, hear my call, Hold my hand lest I fall," the entire congregation was wet with tears, because they knew that they had to cross the River of Jordan. Thus they waited patiently for the familiar lines in the third verse: "At the river I stand, Guide my feet, hold my hand. Take my hand, precious Lord, Lead me home."

It is possible to "have church," as the people would say, without outstanding preaching, but not without good singing. Good singing is indispensable for black worship, for it can fill the vacuum of a poor sermon. There are those who would say that a "good sermon ain't nothing but a song." In recent years, taking their cue from their white counterparts, many black churches have replaced congregational singing with choir singing, thereby limiting the people's involvement in worship. While choirs have their place in certain restricted contexts, the true black service involves the entire congregation in song.

Good singing naturally leads to shouting, which is often evidence that one has been converted. As elements of black worship, shouting and conversion belong together, because they are different moments in a single experience. To shout is to "get happy." It happens in the moment of conversion and in each renewal of that experience in the worshiping community. Shouting is one's response to the movement of the Spirit as one encounters her presence in the worship service. For white intellectuals, including theologians, black folks shouting is perhaps the most bizarre event in their worship services. White intellectuals often identify shouting in the black church with similar events in white churches, trying to give a common sociological and psychological reason for the phenomenon. Such an approach is not only grossly misleading from my theological perspective but also from the premise and procedures that white scholars claim guide their examination. How is it possible to speak of a *common* sociological and psychological reason for religious ecstasy among blacks and whites when they have radically different social and political environments, thereby creating different psychological and religious orientations? It is absurd on sociological, psychological, and theological grounds to contend that the Klu Klux Klansman and the black person who escaped him are shouting for the same or similar reasons in their respective church services. Because whites and blacks have different historical and theological contexts out of which their worship services arise, they do not shout for the same reasons.

The authentic dimension of black people's shouting is found in the joy the people experience when God's Spirit visits their worship and stamps a new identity upon their personhood in contrast to their oppressed status in white society. This and this alone is what the shouting is about. This experience is so radical that the only way to speak of it is in terms of dying and rising again. It is a conversion experience. In one sense conversion is a once-and-for-all event and is associated with baptism. In another sense, one is continually converted anew to the power of the Spirit and this is usually connected with shouting. "God struck me dead," recalled an ex-slave, connecting his conversion with the experience of dying.[5] But on the other side of death is the resurrection, a new life and determination to live for God. Since one cannot stay on the "mountain top" but must return to the "valley of life," there is always the need to return to the place where one once stood in order to experience anew the power of God's Spirit. This is what happens on Sunday morning at the "altar call." The preacher invites the entire congregation to renew their determination to stay on the "Lord's journey" and "to work in his vineyard."

The renewal of one's determination is often done with prayer and testimony. To testify is to stand before the congregation and bear witness to one's determination to keep on the "gospel shoes." "I don't know about you," a sister might say, "but I intend to make it to the end of my journey. I started on this journey twenty-five years ago, and I can't turn back now. I know the way is difficult and the road is rocky. I've been in the valley, and I have a few more mountains to climb. But I want you to know this morning that I ain't going to let a little trouble get in the way of me seeing my Jesus."

Prayer is the final element of black worship to be considered.

---

5. See *God Struck Me Dead*, ed. Clifton Johnson (Philadelphia: Pilgrim Press, 1969).

Like the song, prayer creates the mood for the reception of God's
Spirit and is the occasion when the people specifically request
Jesus to come and be with them. The people actually believe that
they can call Jesus upon the "telephone of prayer" and tell him all
about their troubles. They also contend that his line is never busy,
and he is always ready to receive their call. It is not uncommon to
hear the people say: "Jesus is on the main line, call him up and tell
him what you want." Prayer is a way of communicating with the
divine. That is why a black preacher seldom enters the pulpit
without praying.

Harold Carter, a Baptist preacher in Baltimore, accurately
describes the essence of black prayer: it is "more than a word
spoken; it [is] an event to be experienced. The spirit of what
[happens is] as important as the words [being] spoken."[6] Black
prayer should be heard and not read, because the rhythm of the
language is as crucial to its meaning as is the content of the peti-
tion. To know what black prayer means, one needs to *hear* the
deacon say

> Almighty! and all wise God our heavenly Father!, tis once more
> and again that a few of your beloved children are gathered
> together to call upon your holy name. We bow at your footstool,
> Master, to thank you for our spared lives. We thank you that we
> were able to get up this morning clothed in our right mind. For
> Master, since we met here, many have been snatched out of the
> land of the living and hurled into eternity. But through your
> goodness and mercy we have been spared to assemble ourselves
> here once more to call upon a captain who has never lost a
> battle.[7]

At this point in the prayer, the deacon is ready to go through his
lists of requests, which normally relates to the bestowal of
strength on the people to survive in a sin-sick world. When he
concludes his requests, he moves toward his conclusion.

> And now, oh Lord; when this your humble servant is done
> down here in this low land of sorrow; done sitting down and

6. Carter, *The Prayer Tradition of Black People* (Valley Forge, Pa.: Judson Press,
1976), p. 21.

7. A prayer offered in South Nashville, Tennessee, in the summer of 1928,
reproduced by Langston Hughes and Arna Bontemps in *Book of Negro Folklore*
(New York: Dodd, Mead, 1958), p. 256.

getting up; done being called everything but a child of God; oh, when I am done, done, done, and this old world can afford me a home no longer, right soon in the morning, Lord, right soon in the morning, meet me at the River of Jordan, bid the waters to be still, tuck my little soul away in your chariot, and bear it away over yonder in the third heaven where everyday will be a Sunday and my sorrows of this old world will have an end, is my prayer for Christ my Redeemer's sake and amen and thank God.

If one fact is clear from our examination of black worship, it is primarily a happening in the lives of the people. Both the content of what is said and the manner in which things are expressed emphasize that black worship is an eschatological event, the time when the people experience a liberation in their present that they believe will be fully realized in God's coming future.

Sanctification, Liberation, and the Struggle for Justice

On the basis of our interpretation of black worship as an eschatological event, it is not difficult to understand why Richard Allen, the founder of the African Methodist Episcopal (AME) Church, was so "confident that there was no religious sect or denomination [that] would suit the capacity of the colored people as well as the Methodist."[8] The process of salvation in terms of repentance, forgiveness, and new birth, so important for John Wesley, is also dominant in the black religious tradition generally and black Methodism in particular.[9] Black worship is the actu-

8. Allen, *The Life Experience and Gospel Labors of the Right Reverend Richard Allen* (Nashville: Abingdon Press, 1960), p. 29. For biographies of Allen, see Charles Wesley, *Richard Allen: Apostle of Freedom* (Washington: Associated Publishers, 1935); and Carol V. R. George, *Segregated Sabbaths: Richard Allen and the Emergence of the Independent Black Churches, 1760-1840* (New York: Oxford University Press, 1973).

9. John Wesley's description of the order of salvation emphasizing repentance, justification, new birth, and assurance is prominently present in Richard Allen's account of his conversion experience.

I was awakened and brought to see myself, poor, wretched and undone, and without the mercy of God must be lost. Shortly after, I obtained mercy through the blood of Christ, and was constrained to exhort my old companions to seek the Lord. I went rejoicing for several days and was happy in the Lord, in conversing with many old, experienced Christians. I was brought

alization of the story of salvation as experienced in the lives of oppressed black people.

However, the claim that the black church was influenced by Methodism and other forms of evangelical Protestantism does not mean that there are no essential differences among them. In fact, the differences are perhaps more important than the similarities. That was why Richard Allen and other blacks walked out of St. George Methodist Church of Philadelphia in 1787 and later founded the AME Church in 1816. Similar events happened in other black-white Methodist contexts, giving rise to the AME Zion Church and much later the Colored Methodist Episcopal Church.[10] The central difference between black and white Methodism was and is the refusal of black people to accept racism and

---

under doubts, and was tempted to believe I was deceived, and was constrained to seek the Lord afresh. I went with my head bowed down for many days. My sins were a heavy burden. I was tempted to believe that there was no mercy for me. I cried to the Lord both night and day. One night I thought hell would be my portion. I cried unto Him who delighteth to hear the prayers of a poor sinner, and all of a sudden my dungeon shook, my chains flew off, and, glory to God, I cried. My soul was filled. I cried, enough for me—the Saviour died. My confidence was strengthened that the Lord, of Christ's sake, had heard my prayers and pardoned all my sins. I was constrained to go from house to house, exhorting my old companions, and telling to all round what a dear Savior I had found. (*Life Experience*, pp. 15-16)

The best account of John Wesley's doctrine is still Harold Lindstrom's *Wesley and Sanctification: A Study in the Doctrine of Salvation* (1946; rpt., Grand Rapids: Zondervan, 1983).

10. The best history of black religion is Wilmore's *Black Religion and Black Radicalism*. For a historical account of the rise of black Methodism, see Harry V. Richardson, *Dark Salvation* (New York: Doubleday, 1976). Unfortunately Richardson's book fails to point out the significance of the relation between black faith and history. Careful attention to the theological importance of their relationship would have disclosed the difference between black and white spirituality in Methodism. He seems to be unaware not only of the recent rise of black theology, but also of the *theological* importance of the rise of independent black Methodist churches and also of the emergence of the Black Methodist for Church Renewal (BMCR) in contemporary United Methodism. Robinson includes only one sentence on black theology and one short paragraph on BMCR in the context of about one page on "Protest Movements."

Although it is old, Carter G. Woodson's *History of the Negro Church* (Washington: Associated Publishers, 1945) is still a very important history of the black church. See also my article "Negro Churches (in the United States)" in the *Encyclopaedia Britannica*, 15th ed., 12: 936-37.

social injustice as reconcilable with the experience of conversion and new birth. We do not believe that it is possible to be sanctified and racist at the same time. If conversion and new birth mean anything at all, they must mean the historical actualization of the experience of salvation in works of piety and mercy on behalf of the oppressed of the land. John Wesley seemed to have recognized the historical vocation of the experience of salvation. He not only took a radical stand against slavery[11] but also insisted on the social character of the experience of salvation. "Christianity," wrote Wesley, "is essentially a social religion; and . . . to turn it into a solitary religion is indeed to destroy it."[12] But John Wesley notwithstanding, North American Methodism, unfortunately, did not institutionalize his stand on slavery.[13] The failure of white Methodism in this regard led to the creation of a white spirituality that is culturally determined by American values and thus indifferent to oppressed black people's struggle for social justice.

In contrast, black American spirituality was born in the context of the struggle for justice. The contradiction between the experience of sanctification and human slavery has always been a dominant theme in black religion. It is found not only in the rise of independent black churches but also in our songs, stories, and

11. See his "Thoughts upon Slavery" (1774) in *The Works of John Wesley*, vol. 11 (Grand Rapids: Baker Book, 1981), pp. 59-60.

12. Wesley, cited by Robert F. Wearmouth in *The Social and Political Influence of Methodism in the Twentieth Century* (London: Epworth Press, 1957), p. 185. Despite Wesley's emphasis on the works of piety and mercy, his view of salvation seems to make social justice a secondary ingredient of salvation and at most a mere *consequence* of it.

13. American Methodism began by taking a radical stand on slavery. In 1780 at the Baltimore Conference, the Methodists condemned slavery as "contrary to the laws of God, man, and nature, and hurtful to society." And four years later, at the Christmas Conference of 1784, they "voted to expel all slave-holding of Methodist societies . . . who would not, within twelve months after due notification, perfect a legal document to manumit all their slaves when they reached certain specific ages. The conference also voted to expel immediately all Methodists who bought (except for the purpose of liberation) or sold slaves." However, by the beginning of the nineteenth century, when cotton became king, the Methodists, like other white churches, allowed the change in social reality to influence a change in their stand on slavery. The Methodists suspended their 1784 rules within six months, and in 1816 a General Conference committee reported that "emancipation is impracticable." See H. Shelton Smith, *In His Image, but . . . : Racism in Southern Religion, 1780-1910* (Durham, N.C.: Duke University Press, 1972), pp. 37, 38, 45. For a historical account of Methodism and slavery, see Donald G. Mathews, *Slavery and Methodism* (Princeton: Princeton University Press, 1965).

sermons.[14] When the meaning of sanctification is formed in the social context of an oppressed community in struggle for liberation, it is difficult to separate the experience of holiness from the spiritual empowerment to change the existing societal arrangements. If "I'm a chile of God wid soul set free" because "Christ hab bought my liberty," then I will find it impossible to tolerate slavery and oppression. Black slaves expressed this point in song.

> Oh Freedom! Oh Freedom!
> Oh Freedom, I love thee!
> And before I'll be a slave,
> I'll be buried in my grave,
> And go home to my Lord and be free.

The historical realization of the experience of salvation has always been an integral part of the black religious tradition. The idea that black religion was and is "other-worldly" and nothing more is simply not true. To be sure, black religion is not a social theory that can be a substitute for scientific analysis of societal oppression. But it is a spiritual vision for the reconstruction of a new humanity wherein people are no longer defined by oppression but by freedom. This vision can serve as an important force for organizing people for the transformation of society. Because black people know that they are more than what has been defined for them, this knowledge of the "more" requires that they struggle to realize in the society the freedom they experience in their worship life. Sometimes this experience of God's gift of a new identity actualizes itself in political revolution, as in the well-known insurrections of Gabriel Prosser (1800), Denmark Vesey (1822), and Nat Turner (1831).[15] Black religion is by definition the opposite of white religion because the former was born in the black people's political struggle to liberate themselves from oppression in the white church and the society it justifies. Even when black slaves could not actualize their experience of salvation in

14. For a theological interpretation of the slave songs, often called "Negro Spirituals," see my book *The Spirituals and the Blues.* In my book *God of the Oppressed,* I use the songs, sermons, stories, and prayers as primary sources for a black theology of liberation.

15. See Wilmore's interpretation of these insurrections in chap. 3 of his *Black Religion and Black Radicalism.* For a detailed account of more than two hundred slave revolts, see Herbert Aptheker, *American Negro Slave Revolts* (New York: International Publishers, 1943).

revolutionary struggle, they often verbalized the distinction between black and white religion. "Harriet Martineau recorded the instance of a mistress being told by one of her slaves, 'you no holy. We be holy. You in no state of salvation.'"[16] A similar point is emphasized in a joke about a "slave's reaction to the news that he would be rewarded by being buried in the same vault with his master: 'Well, massa, one way I am satisfied, and one way I am not. I like to have a good coffin when I die [but] I afraid, massa, when the debbil come to take you body, he make mistake, and get mine.'"[17]

Sanctification in black religion cannot be correctly understood apart from black people's struggle for historical liberation. Liberation is not simply a consequence of the experience of sanctification. Rather, sanctification *is* liberation. To be sanctified is to be liberated—that is, politically engaged in the struggle of freedom. When sanctification is defined as a commitment to the historical struggle for political liberation, then it is possible to connect it with socialism and Marxism, the reconstruction of society on the basis of freedom and justice for all.

Although black religion grounds salvation in history and refuses to accept any view of sanctification that substitutes inward piety for social justice, it also includes an eschatological vision. It is important to emphasize that this vision in black religion is derived from Scripture and is not in any sense a rejection of history. To reject history in salvation leads to passivity and makes religion the opiate of the people. Black religion accepts history without limiting salvation to history. As long as people are bound to history, they are bound to law and thus death. If death is the ultimate power, and life has no future beyond this world, then the rulers of the state who control the military take the place of God. They have the future in their hands, and the oppressed can be made to obey the law of injustice. But if the oppressed, while living in history, can see beyond it, if they can visualize an eschatological future beyond this world, then the "sigh of the oppressed creature," to use Marx's phrase, can become a revolutionary cry of rebellion against the established order. It is this revolutionary cry that is granted in the resurrection of Jesus. Salvation then is not

16. Lawrence W. Levine, *Black Culture and Black Consciousness* (New York: Oxford University Press, 1977), p. 34.
17. Cited by Levine in *Black Culture and Black Consciousness*, p. 35.

simply freedom in history; it is freedom to affirm that future
which is beyond history.

Indeed, because we know that death has been conquered, we
are truly free to be human in history, knowing that we have a
"home over yonder." "The home over yonder," vividly and artis-
tically described in the slave songs, is the gift of salvation granted
in the resurrection of Jesus. If we do not take this "otherness" in
salvation with utmost seriousness, then we will have no way to be
sustained in the struggle against injustice. The oppressed will get
tired and also afraid of the risks of freedom. They will say as the
Israelites said to Moses when they found themselves between
Pharaoh's army and the Red Sea, "Is it because there are no
graves in Egypt that you have taken us away to die in the wilder-
ness? What have you done to us, in bringing us out of Egypt?"
(Exod. 14:11). The fear of freedom and the risks contained in
struggle are an ever-present reality. But the "otherness" of salvation, its transcendence beyond history, introduces a factor that
makes a difference. The difference is not that we are taken out of
history while living on earth—that would be an opiate. Rather, it
is a difference that plants our being firmly in history, because we
know that death is not the goal of history. The transcendence
factor in salvation helps us to realize that our fight for justice is
God's fight too, and his presence in Jesus' resurrection has already defined what the ultimate outcome will be. It was this
knowledge that enabled black slaves to live in history but not to be
defeated by their limitations in history. To be sure, they sang
about "rollin' through an unfriendly world," encountering the
terrible reality of pain and death. Death was "a hammer ringin'
on a coffin," "a pale horse an' a rider," "a chariot swingin' low,"
and "a train a-blowin' at de station."

> Same train, same train,
> Same train carry my mother,
> Same train be back tomorrow;
> Same train, same train.

But despite the inevitability and dreadful experience of death,
black slaves refused to accept its ultimacy. They believed that
death had been defeated in Jesus' resurrection.

> When I get to heav'n I will sing and tell,
> How I did shun both death and hell.

Christian Faith and Political Praxis

IN THIS ESSAY, MY CONCERN IS TO EXAMINE THE RELATIONSHIP OF the Christian faith to political praxis, with special reference to the concrete realities of the oppressed and oppressors, whites and blacks, and the church's responsibility to preach and to live the gospel of Jesus Christ in a highly industrialized and capitalistic society.

What is the Christian faith, and what does it have to say about the rich and the poor and the social, economic, and political conditions that determine their relationship? To answer this question is not easy in North America, because we live in a society that claims to separate church and state, religion and politics. "Christianity," it is often said, "is concerned with spiritual reality but not with the material conditions of people." This view of the Christian faith is commonly held both inside and outside of organized churches, thereby supporting the conservative role that religion has often played in politics. If the Christian faith is no more than the cultural and political interests of the rules transformed into theological categories, then Karl Marx is right in his contention that religion is the opium of the people and therefore should be eliminated along with other legitimizing agencies in an oppressive society. But if religion generally and the Christian faith in particular is an imaginative and apocalyptic vision about the creation of a new humanity that is derived from the historical and political struggles of oppressed peoples, then to describe it as a sedative is to misunderstand religion's essential nature and its latent revolutionary and humanizing thrust in society.

When the meaning of Christianity is derived from the bottom

This essay originally was presented at a conference on the "Encounter of Theologies" (Mexico, October 1977) and was reprinted in *Praxis Cristiana y producción teológica*, ed. Jorge V. Pixley and Jean-Pierre Bastian (Salamaca: Ediciones Sigueme, 1979), pp. 75-88. It has also appeared in *Bulletin of African Theology* 2 (1980): 205-18, and *Encounter* 43 (Spring 1982): 129-41.

and not the top of the socio-economic ladder, from people who are engaged in the fight for justice and not from those who seek to maintain the status quo, then something radical and revolutionary happens to the function of the "holy" in the context of the "secular." Viewed from the perspective of oppressed peoples' struggle of freedom, the holy becomes a radical challenge to the legitimacy of the secular structures of power by creating eschatological images about a realm of experience that is not confined to the values of this world. This is the strange and revolutionary character of Christianity that is so often misunderstood by church and nonchurch people alike. When we permit ourselves to experience the root meaning of the biblical message and to hear the claims that it lays upon all who would dare be Christian in this world, then we will see the radical difference between the established churches and the truth of the gospel. For inherent in the Christian gospel is the refusal to accept the things that are as the things that ought to be. This "great refusal" is what makes Christianity what it is and thus infuses in its very nature a radicality that can never accept the world as it is.

This radical perspective of the biblical faith has not always been presented as an essential part of the Christian gospel. At least since the time when the Emperor Constantine made Christianity the official religion of the Roman State, the chief interpreters of the Christian tradition have advocated a spiritual view of the gospel that separates the confession of faith from the practice of political justice. Whether we speak of Augustine's identification of slavery with the sins of the slaves, Luther's stand against the Peasants' Revolt, the white American church's endorsement of black slavery, or contemporary Euro-American theology's indifference toward the political embodiment of the gospel, it is unquestionably clear that the dominant representatives of the Christian tradition, both Protestant and Catholic, have contributed to the political oppression of humanity by defending the economic interests of the rich against the poor. When the gospel is spiritualized so as to render invisible the important economic distinctions between the haves and the have-nots, the dialectical relation between faith and the practice of political justice is also obscured.

Recently the assumed separation between faith and political praxis has been seriously challenged by the appearance of liberation theologies in North and South America, Africa, and Asia.

Whether we speak of black theology, feminist theology, or African theology, liberation theology in all forms rejects the dichotomy between spiritual and physical salvation, between faith and political praxis, and insists on their dialectical relationship. Liberation theology has been created by people who consciously seek to speak to and for the victims of economic and political injustice as represented in racism, classism, and sexism. The advocates of this new theology are intolerant of any perspective on Christianity that fails to relate the gospel of Jesus to the economic and social conditions of people. They contend that the gospel embraces the whole person in human society, in work and play. This means that the gospel is inseparably connected with the bodily liberation of the poor.

Because I am a black North American theologian whose political and religious consciousness has been shaped in and by black people's historical fight for justice, I agree with my theological colleagues in Africa, Asia, and Latin America who contend that the gospel cannot be separated from the concrete struggles of freedom among the oppressed of the land. Indeed, this theological conviction has been an integral part of the black religious tradition from its beginning,[1] and it was reinforced in my theological consciousness during the civil rights movement and in the context of the rise of Black Power. The civil rights movement of the 1950s and '60s, which was created and largely centered in the black churches with Martin Luther King, Jr., as its charismatic leader, demonstrated the continuing relevancy of black religion in the struggle for political and social justice. Not only were political strategy sessions held in the context of church worship, but many black ministers withdrew from formal denominational ties in order to devote full time to sit-ins, "freedom rides," and other political activities. But the increasing violence of the existing structures of North American society, as well as black people's determination to assert their freedom in opposition to it, led many black civil rights workers to question King's uncompromising devotion to the principle of nonviolence. Thus, in the context

1. The best historical account of the black religious tradition is that of Gayraud S. Wilmore, in chap. 4 of his *Black Religion and Black Radicalism* (Garden City, N.Y.: Doubleday, 1972). For other historical accounts of black religion in North America, see chap. 2 of Cecil Cone's *The Identity Crisis in Black Theology* (Nashville: AMEC, 1975), and Joseph Washington's *Black Religion* (Boston: Beacon, 1964).

of the James Meredith March in Mississippi (spring 1966), and in light of many years of the carefully organized violence by white societal structures, Willie Ricks sounded the cry of Black Power, and Stokely Carmichael and others enthusiastically accepted the intellectual challenge to define its political and social relevance in American society.[2]

Black theology was born in response to the rise of Black Power and in the context of the National Committee of Negro Churchmen.[3] From the beginning, black theology was interpreted as the theological arm of Black Power with the responsibility to define the religious meaning of our prior political commitment to black liberation. The initial move in this direction was the publication of the "Black Power" statement (July 1966),[4] in which an ecumenical group of black churchmen defended the right of black people to empower themselves against the encroachment of white racism. Following the publication of the "Black Power" statement, many black church people began to move away from King's rigid commitment to nonviolence and to express their solidarity with James Forman's Marxist and revolutionary "Black Manifesto."[5] Although we respected the integrity of King's commitment to the struggle for justice, we nevertheless felt that his nonviolent method for radical change in societal structures was

2. For an account of the rise of Black Power, see Stokely Carmichael and Charles V. Hamilton, *Black Power: The Politics of Liberation in America* (New York: Random House, 1967); for Martin Luther King's response to Black Power, see his *Where Do We Go From Here: Chaos or Community?* (New York: Harper & Row, 1967).

3. The National Committee of Negro Churchmen was an ad hoc ecumenical group of black ministers that was later formalized into a permanent body under the name National Conference of Black Christians (NCBC), with headquarters in Atlanta, Georgia. This was the principal black church organization that struggled to respond to the creative politics of Black Power.

4. This statement originally appeared as an advertisement in *The New York Times*. It was the first of a series of policy statements issued by NCBC to help to define the political direction of the black church in the 1960s and '70s. Most of these documents are reprinted in Warner Traynham's *Christian Faith in Black and White: A Primer in Theology from the Black Perspective* (Boston: Parameter Press, 1973).

5. Perhaps no document or person disturbed the religious complacency of the white and black churches more than Forman and his "Black Manifesto." For an interpretation of this document and the events surrounding it, see Arnold Schuchter's *Reparations: The Black Manifesto and Its Challenge to White America* (Philadelphia: Lippincott, 1970).

not radical enough and was too dependent upon the possibility of change in the hearts of white oppressors. The problem with King's assumption was that it did not take seriously enough Henry H. Garnet's claim that "if [slaves] would be free, they must themselves strike the blow."[6]

The theological meaning of Garnet's assertion for black Christians had to be worked out in the historical context of white violence. As black people were being systematically exterminated through American military structures (dramatically symbolized in the abortive insurrections in Watts, Detroit, and Newark), we black theologians had to ask what the gospel has to do with life and death and the struggle of people to be free in an extreme situation of oppression. The existential and political implications of this question forced us to take a new look at the theological enterprise, and we concluded that the beginning and the end of the Christian faith is found in the struggle for justice on behalf of the victims of oppressive societal structures. Whatever else Christian theology might be, it must take sides with the victims who are economically and politically oppressed. If theology does not side with the victims of economic injustice, it cannot represent *the Victim,* Jesus of Nazareth, who was crucified because he was a threat to the political and religious structures of his time. That insight impressed itself on our consciousness to such a degree that we began to speak of a black theology of liberation.[7] Our central concern was to show that the Christian faith, as lived by oppressed people generally, and oppressed black people in particular, has been—and more importantly *can be*—an instrument of economic and political freedom.

It is out of the historical context of the black church's identification of the Christian gospel with the political liberation of the poor that I would like to say a word about faith and work, the-

6. See Garnet's "Address to the Slaves of the United Statesof America" (1843), reprinted in *Walker's "Appeal" and Garnet's "Address to the Slaves of the United States of America,"* by Henry H. Garnet and David Walker, American Negro: His History and Literature Series (New York: Arno Press, 1969).

7. The first book on "black theology" was my *Black Theology and Black Power* (New York: Seabury Press, 1969). Although the theme of liberation is present in that volume, the theological focus of the theme appeared in my second volume, *A Black Theology of Liberation* (Philadelphia: Lippincott, 1970). Other books on black theology include J. Deotis Roberts's *Liberation and Reconciliation: A Black Theology* (Philadelphia: Westminster Press, 1971); Cecil Cone's *Identity Crisis in Black Theology;* and my *God of the Oppressed* (New York: Seabury Press, 1975).

ology and the practice of political justice. In this essay, I will try to
state what faith demands of praxis and what praxis demands of
faith. The discussion will proceed with a description of faith in
the context of black theology and then to an examination of the
praxis inherent in that faith.

Faith in Christ the Liberator

Faith is a religious term that expresses a person's commitment to
the ultimate. According to Paul Tillich, "faith is a total and centered act of the personal self, the act of unconditional, infinite
and ultimate concern."[8] In its broadest theological sense, faith
may refer to one's commitment to things of this world or be more
narrowly limited to a commitment to God in the context of organized religion. The distinctive characteristic of faith is its total
commitment to that which functions as the ultimate in one's life,
giving it order and meaning. Faith is that total commitment which
gives a people its identity and thus determines what they must do
in order to actualize in society what they believe necessary for the
attainment of their peoplehood.

When faith is understood as commitment to an ultimate concern, then it is obvious that there can be no separation between
faith and obedience, because obedience determines faith. I know
what your faith is *not* by what you confess but *only* by what you do.
I will say more about this particular point when I turn to a discussion of praxis. At this juncture, I merely want to emphasize that
the very nature of faith demands a practical activity commensurate with its confession.

In light of this general definition of faith, we might best define
Christian faith as that total commitment arising from Jesus of
Nazareth: his life, death, and resurrection. Faith, as defined in
the Christian context, is not belief in propositional truths designated as important by organized churches; rather, it is an ultimate commitment to a particular God who revealed the fullness
of divinity in the human presence of Jesus Christ.

In order to clarify the sociological content of my theological
affirmation, it is necessary to state the source of my faith perspective. My view of the Christian gospel is derived from the biblical
message as interpreted in the liberation struggle of an oppressed

8. Tillich, *Dynamics of Faith* (New York: Harper & Row, 1958), p. 8.

North American black community and reinforced by similar interpretations among oppressed peoples fighting for freedom throughout the world. From the dialectical relationship of these historical contexts arises the theological conviction that the Bible is the story of God's liberation of victims from economic and political oppression. Historically, the story begins with the liberation of Israelite slaves from Egypt and the establishment of the covenant at Sinai.

> You have seen what I did to the Egyptians, and how I bore you on eagles' wings and brought you to myself. *Now therefore,* if you will obey my voice and keep my covenant, you shall be my own possession among all peoples; for all the earth is mine, and you shall be to me a kingdom of priests and a holy nation.
>
> Exodus 19:4-5, RSV

In the Old Testament, faith in God is based on a historical event of rescue wherein Israelite slaves became God's free people with the responsibility of spreading freedom throughout the land. Faith is accepting the gift of freedom and putting one's absolute trust in the promise of God to be with the little ones in time of distress. When Israel lapsed from this faith in God's righteousness and forgot its slave heritage by treating the poor unjustly, divine love was transformed into wrath. The God of the Old Testament is the God of justice whose revelation is identical with the liberation of the oppressed. For the basic human sin is the attempt to be God, to take his place by ordering the societal structures according to one's political interests. Sin is not primarily a religious impurity but rather social, political, and economic oppression of the poor. It is the denial of the humanity of the neighbor through unjust political and economic arrangements. When the prophets lay God's demands before the kings and priests of Israel, the demand is identical with justice for the poor and the weak. A faith that expresses itself in rituals is not enough:

> I hate, I despise your feasts,
>   and I take no delight in your solemn assemblies.
> Even though you offer me your burnt offerings and cereal
>   offerings,
>   I will not accept them,
> and the peace offerings of your fatted beasts
>   I will not look upon.

Take away from me the noise of your songs;
  to the melody of your harp I will not listen.
But let justice roll down like waters,
  and righteousness like an over-flowing stream.
                                    Amos 5:21-24, RSV

Amos and other prophets contended that Israel would be sent back to servitude not because the people failed to attend religious services but because of their *economic* oppression of the poor.

The same theme of God's solidarity with the victim is found in the New Testament, where it receives a universal expression in the particularity of Jesus' life, death, and resurrection. The appearance of Jesus as the Oppressed One prevents any easy identification with his ministry. Jesus was not a successful person by North American standards. Neither was he morally good and religiously respected. He identified with the prostitutes and drunkards, the unemployed and the poor—not because he felt sorry for them, but in order to reveal God's judgment against social and religious structures that oppress the weak. Jesus was born like the poor, he lived with them, and on the cross he died like them. If Jesus is the divine revelation of God's intention for humanity, then faith is nothing but trust in the One who came in Christ for the liberation of the poor. To place one's trust in this God means that one's value-system is no longer derived from the established structures of the world but from one's struggle against these unjust structures.

It is significant that the biblical theme of God's solidarity with the historical liberation of the oppressed was notably absent in the songs and sermons of white missionaries when they introduced their version of Christianity to African slaves in North America. Like all oppressors who interpret the gospel in the light of their assumption that they have a right to dominate others, white preachers contended that God willed Africans to be slaves, and they cited such biblical references as Noah's curse upon Ham and the apostle Paul's injunction "slaves be obedient to your masters" as the theological justification of their claim. But black slaves rejected the white distortions of the gospel and insisted that God willed their freedom and not their slavery. As evidence, they pointed to the Exodus, the prophets, and Jesus' preaching of the gospel to the poor and not the rich. Through sermons, prayers, and songs, black slaves created a version of Christianity qualitatively different from that of their masters. The distinctiveness of black faith is its focus on God's will to liberate those who are oppressed. That is why the independent black churches were created in the North and the "invisible" (secret) churches were formed in the South. Black people were determined to fashion a faith that was identical with their political fight for justice. In the ecstasy of their church services was born their encounter with the God of Moses and Jesus, and he bestowed upon them the power to actualize in their present history the freedom they experienced in their worship and read about in the Scriptures.

> Oh Freedom! Oh Freedom!
> Oh Freedom, I love thee!
> And before I'll be a slave,
> I'll be buried in my grave,
> And go home to my Lord and be free.[9]

The historical embodiment of black faith is found not only in the creation of separate institutional black churches with songs, prayers, and sermons about liberation. Also important is the presence of black faith outside of the confessional and organizational framework of black denominations. Black faith is found in "secular" songs and stories, slave insurrections, and protest assemblies. When I speak of black faith, I am referring only secondarily to organized religion and primarily to black people's collective acknowledgment of the spirit of liberation in their midst, a Spirit who empowers them to struggle for freedom even though the odds are against them. This is the historical matrix out of which my hermeneutical perspective has been formed.

Since other oppressed peoples in and outside of North America are making similar claims regarding God's solidarity with the poor, the North American black perspective is reinforced and enlarged. Indeed, the universal dimension of the biblical faith, so central in the New Testament, is found in God's will to make liberation not simply the property of one people but of all hu-

9. For a theological interpretation of the black spirituals in particular and black religion generally, see my study *The Spirituals and the Blues* (New York: Seabury Press, 1972).

mankind. Wherever people are being dehumanized, divine righteousness is disclosed in their historical struggle to be other than what is intended by oppressive rulers.

Faith, then, is a human response to the liberating presence of the divine Spirit in an oppressed community. God's Spirit is liberating because she gives people the courage and power to resist dehumanization and slavery. Through faith, oppressed people receive the gift of a new humanity that can be realized only in the historical process of liberation. But since faith does not have included in its confession the social analysis needed to implement its eschatological vision of freedom, it must relate itself to a social theory in order to actualize in society what it confesses in worship. This leads us to an analysis of praxis.

Faith and Praxis

In philosophical and theological circles, *praxis* is a term closely related to the philosophy of Karl Marx. It is perhaps best summarized in Marx's often-quoted eleventh thesis on Feuerbach: "The philosophers have only *interpreted* the world in various ways; the point however is to change it."[10] Praxis is that directed activity toward freedom wherein people recognize that truth is not primarily a question of theory but a practical question. In practice people must prove the truth by destroying the existing relations of untruth. As Gajo Petrović says, *"The question of the essence of freedom . . . is not only a question. It is at once participation in the production of freedom. It is an activity through which freedom frees itself."*[11]

In a broad sense, praxis is connected with the Christian idea of obedience and is identical with the horizontal implementation of the vertical dimension of faith. According to the New Testament, Jesus says, "Not every one who says to me, 'Lord, Lord,' shall enter the kingdom of heaven, but he who does the will of my Father who is in heaven" (Matt. 7:21, RSV). A similar point is made in 1 John. "He who does right is righteous. . . . If any one says, 'I love God,' and hates his brother [or sister], he is a liar; for he

---

10. Marx, in *Marx and Engels: Basic Writings on Politics and Philosophy* (Garden City, N.Y.: Doubleday, 1959), p. 120.

11. Petrović, *Marx in the Mid-Twentieth Century* (Garden City, N.Y.: Doubleday, 1967), p. 120.

who does not love his brother [or sister] whom he has seen, cannot love God whom he has not seen" (3:7; 4:20, RSV). Inherent in the biblical faith is the obedience that defines it. In contemporary theology, no one made this point any clearer than Dietrich Bonhoeffer: *"Only he who believes is obedient, and only he who is obedient believes."* He goes on to say, "It is quite unbiblical to hold the first proposition without the second. . . . Faith is only real when there is obedience, never without it, and faith only becomes faith in the act of obedience." Therefore he says, "Only the obedient believe. . . . Without this preliminary step of obedience, our faith is only a pious humbug, and leads us to grace which is not costly."[12]

In North America, black slaves' perception of this biblical insight enabled them to make the distinction between the confession of faith and the obedience that validated it. They knew that their slavery invalidated white religion. That's why they sang "Everybody talking about heaven ain't going there." Some slaves even contended that "No white people went to heaven."[13] On one occasion a white minister's sermon was interrupted by an elderly slave with the question: "Is us slaves gonna be free in Heaven?" The white preacher paused with surprise and anger. But Uncle Silas was persistent: "Is God gonna free us slaves when we get to Heaven?" The remainder of the incident was described by a slave who was present:

> Old white preacher pult out his handkerchief an' wiped de sweat fum his face. "Jesus says come unto Me ye who are free frum sin an' I will give you salvation." "Gonna give us freedom 'long wid salvation?" asked Uncle Silas. "De Lawd gives an' de Lawd takes away, and he dat is widdout sin is gonna have life everlastin'," preached the preacher. Den he went ahead preachin', fast-like, widdout payin' no 'tention to Uncle Silas.[14]

Uncle Silas was insisting on the practical implications of faith which the white preacher had no intention of granting, especially in view of the economic and political consequences.

12. Dietrich Bonhoeffer, *The Cost of Discipleship* (New York: Macmillan, 1961), pp. 54, 55.
13. Cited by Lawrence Levine in *Black Culture and Black Consciousness: Afro-American Folk Thought from Slavery to Freedom* (New York: Oxford University Press, 1977), p. 34.
14. Cited by Levine in *Black Culture and Black Consciousness,* p. 46.

Because oppressors do not reorder the structures of society on the basis of an appeal to the practical implications of faith, praxis is more than the biblical understanding of obedience. And it is this "more" that gives it its distinctive identity. Praxis is a specific kind of obedience that organizes itself around a social theory of reality in order to implement in society the freedom inherent in faith. If faith is the belief that God created all for freedom, then praxis is the social theory used to analyze the structures of injustice so that we will know what must be done for the historical realization of freedom. To sing about freedom and to pray for its coming is not enough. Freedom must be actualized in history by oppressed peoples who accept the intellectual challenge to analyze the world for the purpose of changing it.

The focus on praxis for the purpose of societal change is what distinguishes Marx from Hegel, liberation theology from other theologies of freedom. That is why Marx studied the economic forces in society and why liberation theologians in Latin America find his social theory so basic in the development of their theological enterprise. For the same reason, black liberation theologians also connect their theological program to social theories about racism. Feminist theologians do the same in their analysis of sexism. While there are different emphases among liberation theologians regarding the major historical contradiction in society, they all agree with the need to relate theology to a social theory of reality, because they share the conviction that truth is found in the active transformation of unjust societal structures.

For liberation theologians, faith and praxis belong together, because faith can be expressed only in a political commitment to the humanization of society. We believe that inherent in faith is the love of God, and the latter can be manifested only in the love of the neighbor. Therefore Gustavo Gutiérrez writes that "to know God is to do justice." He continues, "It is not enough to say that the love of God is inseparable from the love of one's neighbor. It must be added that the love for God is unavoidably expressed through love of one's neighbor."[15] But in order to protect love from sentimentality, we must analyze it in the fabric of social relationships where people are situated, in their economic, cultural, and racial coordinates. What does it mean to love

15. Gutiérrez, *A Theology of Liberation* (Maryknoll, N.Y.: Orbis, 1973), p. 200.

the exploited social classes, the dominated people or a marginalized race?

It is in the attempt to answer this question that we also realize that praxis is inseparably connected with faith that expresses itself in love of the neighbor. If the masses are our neighbors, then we will find it impossible to tolerate economic structures that are destructive to their humanity. Love demands justice—that is, the creation of a space in the world so that love can realize itself in human relations. To love the neighbor requires more than a pious feeling in my heart. It requires social and political analysis so that piety will not become a substitute for justice.

The truth of the gospel, then, is a truth that must be done and not simply spoken. To speak the truth without doing the truth is to contradict the truth one claims to affirm. The church is good at writing resolutions and preaching sermons against this or that idea, but the denunciation of injustice is not only a spoken "word" or a written "text." "It is an action, a stand."[16] The word is only a gesture of commitment. This gesture must be concretized by the social analysis so that the oppressed will be empowered to challenge the unjust societal arrangements.

Faith actualized through love can be concretized only by connecting faith with the praxis of justice. The theological assumption that necessitates the connection of faith with praxis is found in Jesus Christ. The incarnation connects faith with life and work. By becoming human in Jesus, God connects faith with the social, political, and economic conditions of people and establishes the theological conclusion that we cannot be faithful to the Creator without receiving the political command to structure creation according to freedom.

The best way to understand the relation of faith and praxis is to reverse the order as seen in Bonhoeffer's contention that "only the obedient believe." To be sure, ontologically faith is prior to obedience and thus is its foundation. But practically obedience comes before faith. We do not first receive faith from God or the church and then seek to live that faith in the world. It is the other way around. One meets God in the process of historical liberation. In the historical context of the struggle for freedom, one receives the gift of divine freedom wherein the realization occurs

16. Gutiérrez, *A Theology of Liberation*, p. 268.

that the eternal structures of creation are empowering the oppressed in their fight for justice. This realization is the gift of
faith.

Faith, then, is not a datum but a commitment that arises out of
the struggle for freedom and not before. The power that throws
us in the struggle for freedom before we consciously see its connection with faith may be called the prevenient grace of God.
This grace is ontologically prior to justification and sanctification
because it is grounded in the creative will of God. Therefore,
when we are justified and sanctified by the grace of God, the
recognition of both experiences occurs in the struggle of freedom, and it is a gift of God.

By putting obedience prior to faith on the sociological plane,
we protect ourselves from the heresy of substituting faith for
action. We must never allow a prayer for justice to replace an act
against injustice. But if our act against oppression is to have
meaning and not be purposeless, then obedience must connect
itself with a social theory of change. *Why* are people poor, and *who*
benefits from their poverty? In an attempt to answer this question, theology must actualize its Christian identity through social
analysis and political participation on behalf of the victims of
economic justice.

When theology defines the meaning of Christian obedience in
terms structured in sociology and politics, it becomes global in its
outlook by analyzing international capitalism and multinational
corporations. For what oppressors do to the poor in North America, they also do to poor countries. The world becomes their
domain for economic exploitation. Holiday Inn, Gulf Oil, and
other multinational corporations are present in South Africa and
other Third World countries exploiting the victims. Anyone who
would be Christian by taking a stand with the victims should
connect obedience with praxis—that is, with a social theory of
change that will disclose both the causes of injustice and what
must be done to eliminate it.

However, those who would cast their lot with the victims must
not forget that the existing structures are powerful and complex.
Their creators intend them to be that way, so that any action that
challenges their existence will appear both immoral and useless.
Oppressors want people to think that change is impossible. That
is the function of the military. They want to scare the victims so
that any social and political analysis will lead to despair. This is

what King called the "paralysis of analysis." But the truth is otherwise: if analysis does not elicit hope for change, then it is incorrect, for the constituent definition of humanity is that people are agents of history, capable of changing the world.

Because hope is the foundation of praxis, praxis can never be separated from faith. The Christian faith is grounded in the promise of God and is actualized in the process of liberation in history. Praxis without faith leads to despair. Despair is the logical consequence of a praxis that does not know the eschatological hope derived from historical struggle. Without hope, there is no struggle. It was this eschatological knowledge, derived from Jesus' cross and resurrection, that enabled black North American slaves to struggle in history but not to be defeated by their historical limitations. To be sure, they sang about the fear of "sinking down" and the dread of being a "motherless child." They experienced trouble and the agony of being alone where "I couldn't hear nobody pray." They encountered death and expressed it in song:

> Soon one mornin', death comes a creepin' in my room.
> O my Lawd, O my Lawd, what shall I do?
> Death done been here, took my mother an' gone,
> O my Lawd, what shall I do?

In these songs are expressed the harsh realities of history and the deep sense of dread at the very thought of death. But because the slaves believed that death had been conquered in Jesus' resurrection, they could also transcend death by interpreting salvation as a heavenly, eschatological reality. That was why they also sang

> You needn't mind my dying,
> Jesus' goin' to make up my dying bed.
> In my room I know,
> Somebody is going to cry,
> All I ask you to do for me,
> Just close my dying eyes.

This is not passive resignation but rather an eschatological expression of a historical commitment that refuses to adjust itself to the power of oppressors. This is what the praxis of faith in a Christian context is all about.

A Theological Challenge to the American Catholic Church

I AM NEITHER CATHOLIC NOR OF EUROPEAN DESCENT. MOREOVER, I cannot speak for blacks or other minorities in the Catholic Church, because I am a Protestant, though my Protestantism is defined more by the faith of African slaves of nineteenth-century America than by the theology of the sixteenth-century Protestant Reformation. Therefore my perspective on the Catholic Church may sound strange to persons whose idea of justice is defined primarily by the dominant theological traditions of Europe and America. What I have to say may appear unnecessarily harsh and insensitive to persons unfamiliar with the struggle for justice in African-American history and culture.

I will not try to be "objective" and "fair" in my analysis, because these terms are often used by the powerful in order to control the words and actions of their victims in the struggle for justice. If I overstate my argument or fail to give appropriate recognition to many deserving Catholics, I ask in advance that my oversight be attributed to the limitation of time for preparation, the lack of first-hand knowledge of Catholic ecclesiastical structures, and particularly to the depth of my concern for the establishment of racial justice in American society and its churches. I do not claim to speak the last word regarding the Catholic Church, justice, and black people. I merely hope that what I say today arises from the truth of the gospel to which we are all accountable.

When a black liberation theologian looks at the Catholic Church, there are many ambivalent reactions. On the one hand, the Catholic Church is the largest single denomination in the United States, and has been one of the most progressive churches regarding the nuclear freeze and in its support of the struggles of

---

This essay was originally presented at the "Voices for Justice" Conference held at the College of Notre Dame in Baltimore, in July 1983.

the poor for justice in Latin America. On the other hand, the Catholic Church is unprogressive and often reactionary regarding the problem of racism in the church and the society. It is clear that justice for African-Americans has not been and is not today a major priority for most white Catholics, even among liberation-oriented persons. For example, why are liberation-oriented Catholics so silent about racism in American society and its churches and so supportive of the struggles of the poor for justice in Latin America? What does this contradiction tell us about the Catholic idea of justice?

I am currently [summer 1983] teaching at the Institute of Justice and Peace at Maryknoll School of Theology, and I have been shocked by the paucity of information available on black history and culture in contrast to the vast amount of library materials on Latin America. When I reflected upon my experiences at other Catholic institutions, discussing the issue of racial justice with black Catholics, it became clear to me that Maryknoll is not unique in terms of its failure to incorporate courses on black history and culture into its curriculum. Indeed, Maryknoll is quite progressive in this regard when compared with most Catholic institutions.

Why are most Catholics, many of whom say that they are concerned about justice, so uninformed about the struggle for justice in black history and culture? What does this ignorance mean when there are more than one million blacks in the Catholic Church and nearly thirty million in the United States? Do white Catholics think that they can have a genuine concern for justice independent of a concern for the elimination of racism in the churches and the world? Do they think that they can develop a method for the elimination of injustice without a keen knowledge of the history and culture of blacks in the United States? Must not the victims of racial injustice have some input into the Catholic definition of justice and also in developing an adequate method for establishing it?

Even more serious than white Catholics' ignorance about the history of the black struggle for justice is the absence of any concern about it among most liberals and radicals, many of whom are working in the black community, teaching our children and influencing their parents. Unfortunately, many whites honestly believe that their choice to work in the black community, with all the disadvantages associated with urban ghettos, is itself proof that they are not racists and thus do not need to study black history and culture in order to be effective liberators in the ghetto. When whites connect their vocational choice with divine revelation, as is often the case with Catholics, they become dogmatic, not only in their opinions about the gospel but also regarding God's will for black people.

One example in this regard is something that happened to me recently. A white Catholic radical talked to me about a Catholic high school in a large city where ninety percent of the students were black and nearly all the teachers were white. During our conversation, his major concern was the middle-class values of the black students, the fear that, in effect, he was "blacker" than they or any of their parents. I always get a little upset when whites tell me that they are "more black" in their values than some blacks whom they know, as if the meaning of blackness is easily assessable by the descendants of slavemasters after a little reading and a brief tenure in the ghetto.

Since he taught U.S. history and other related subjects at that high school, I asked him whether he included materials about African-Americans in his courses and whether there were any courses in the curriculum that specifically focused on their history and culture? His answer to both concerns was negative. I then asked how he could teach the truth about U.S. history without dealing with the history of slavery and segregation and black people's struggle to achieve justice in the land of their birth? How could he teach *black* students, with human sensitivity and a Christian commitment to justice, and not develop courses that focus primarily on their history and culture? Does not the absence of materials about and by blacks mean that they are regarded as insignificant participants in human history? I told him that he, like so many well-intended white radicals, was teaching racism. Indeed, it is sad to say that most educational institutions (both religious and secular, white and some black ones too!) teach racism through what they exclude from the content of their curriculum, the racial identity of the majority of their teachers and students, and the social and religious values that they advocate.

No student should be able to graduate from any high school, college, university, or seminary without being *required* to study under, with, and about blacks. To allow blacks to remain invisible in the study of humanity merely encourages self-hate among blacks and reinforces racism among whites. Justice in the churches and the society must include cultural and historical recognition for all races and ethnic groups. Without the basic recognition of a people's humanity, genuine dialogue and mutual respect and support of each other in the struggle for justice cannot be achieved.

Education should help persons of different races and cultures to get along with each other so they can work together toward the building of a more humane and just society. But how can institutions educate people to respect the humanity of blacks if they teach that only white people's history is worthy of serious scholarly reflection? For white Catholics to claim that the invisibility of blacks in their theology and history is an innocent oversight only demonstrates how deeply racism is embedded in their church and the society. But whether intentional or not, such distinctions do not make the consequences of injustice any less painful to the victims.

Can anyone imagine an educational institution in which the students are ninety percent white and the teachers are virtually all black with a curriculum focusing exclusively on black history and culture? Absolutely not! When I finished telling that white Catholic teacher about the nature of his own racism and his contribution to what he called the middle-class values in black students, he became conspiciously silent and unresponsive to my concerns, thereby confirming that he was unprepared to reflect seriously upon his racism with the intention of correcting it.

His unwillingness to ponder my sharp criticisms was not surprising. In fact, most liberal and radical whites are only concerned about justice from the perspective of their own history and tradition and not from the vantage point of the history and culture of the victims, especially those of African descent. Whether liberal, conservative, or radical, there is one thing that most whites have in common: they act as if whites know everything, and they are therefore seldom open to learning anything from black history and culture. The token presence of blacks may be useful in providing a little variety for those who happen to be interested in cultural pluralism. For example, blacks are especially useful as singers, dancers, and preachers at the Mass and in other liturgical settings.

But when Catholics think about theology and ethical concepts of justice, they assume that blacks are incapable of making any significant contribution. That is why most white Catholics do not know or care to know anything about black theology. Theology is for people capable of metaphysical reflections about God, Jesus, the Holy Spirit, and the church. For serious theological reflections, past or present, Catholics turn to Thomas Aquinas, Karl Rahner, Johann Baptist Metz, Edward Schillebeeckz, Hans Küng, and others like them. If they should happen to have a strong interest in justice, they may turn to Latin American liberation theologians—but not to black Catholic theologians in the United States.

I know that many liberal and radical white Catholics would vehemently deny that they hold such beliefs. But their actions say otherwise. Why are there so few black Catholic theologians teaching in major Catholic colleges, universities, and seminaries? For example, I was told that a *major* Catholic university did not have *one* full-time black teacher on its faculty, not to mention teachers of theology. When asked about this serious educational flaw, the responsible authorities said that they could not find any "qualified" blacks. That officials of Catholic schools are still making such statements in the 1980s only reveals the pervasiveness of the racism that continues to define the behavior of the churches and their institutions. Not even secular universities and colleges can get away with such blatant racist remarks. Unfortunately, the university in question is not unique; it represents the values of the American Catholic Church itself.

The only place where blacks' presence seems to dominate in white schools is on the basketball court and the football field. When it comes to faculty and students with exceptional academic promise, blacks are seldom found in any significant numbers. Why is it that white college and university officials know how to recruit talented black basketball and football players but claim that they do not know how to find gifted black students and faculty? Why are white Catholic liberals and radicals silent about it? What is at stake in this silence? What is it about the Catholic definition of justice that makes many persons of that faith progressive in their attitude toward the poor in Central America but reactionary in their views toward the poor in black America? Unless the conference participants face these questions honestly, I am afraid that the Catholic idea of justice will continue to sound like strange music to the ears of black people.

From the perspective of a black liberation theologian, the Catholic Church is a racist church, and even its most progressive people are seldom bothered by it. It is the failure of the Catholic Church to deal effectively with the problem of racism that causes me to question the quality of its commitment to justice in other areas. I do not wish to minimize the importance of Catholic contributions to poor people's struggles for justice, but I must point out the *ambiguity* of the Catholic stand on justice when racism is not addressed forthrightly. The racism about which I speak is easy for whites to ignore, because they are not its victims and because its dehumanizing consequences are less visible than the racist acts in Mississippi and Alabama during the 1960s or in present-day South Africa. Racism among white Catholics is similar to the racism among white Protestants: it is sophisticated in that it can best be defined by black invisibility in Catholic theology and history. There are very few white Catholic theologians, priests, and sisters who think that knowledge of black history and culture is indispensable for an adequate understanding of justice in this society and the world.

What I have said about the Catholic Church can be said also about white Protestant denominations—but with one significant exception. The Catholic hierarchy in the United States is exclusively controlled by whites. Many black Catholics, therefore, find it difficult to challenge structures of authority in the church without enormous limitations being placed on their ministry. This may be one of the chief reasons why I was invited to make this presentation today. As a Protestant in an independent black denomination that was founded as the African Methodist Episcopal Church in 1816, I am free to tell you what I think with no fear of reprisals from a white ecclesiastical structure.

Black Catholics, whose identity is strongly influenced by their own history and culture, know existentially the contradiction of being both black and Catholic. These two realities are not easily held together in one person, because the Catholic side is very inflexible and thus refuses to be significantly informed by the black experience. Many blacks cannot reconcile both realities and opt for only one of them. Some choose blackness and leave the Catholic Church. Others choose the Catholic side and sever their relationship with the black community. It is difficult to distinguish the values and behavior of such persons from their white counterparts. As C. Eric Lincoln put it, "Blacks who found care in the white man's church, or who accepted spiritual care and oversight under the aegis of the white man's religion, soon found themselves inevitably more sympathic to the white man's plans for non-whites."

However, it is important to point out that there are some black Catholics who refuse to deny their blackness; they refuse to accept European values as the exclusive definition of the Catholic Church. Like many blacks in white Protestant churches, these black Catholics openly acknowledge the pervasive presence of racism in the church. But they are determined to extend the definition of "catholic" to its true meaning—a *universality* defined by the theological reflections and cultures of all people. They appreciate the Catholic Church's public declarations against racism as found in its "Discrimination and Christian Conscience" (1958), "National Race Crisis" (1968), and "Brothers and Sisters to Us: Bishops' Pastoral Letter on Racism in Our Day" (1979). But black Catholics know that such statements mean very little unless they are backed up with radical actions commensurate with the depth of the problem. What does it mean for Catholic bishops to say that "racism is an evil which endures in our society and in our Church" and then to do almost nothing to eliminate it? It may be difficult for the bishops to eliminate racism in society, especially in light of the principle of the separation of church and state, but they should be able to reduce racism considerably in their own church. Why are there so few black bishops, and why are most of them without any significant power? The last count I heard was seven black bishops, only one of whom is an ordinary! There are fewer than four hundred black priests and a few more than six hundred sisters for more than one million black Catholics! What does this information say to blacks about the Catholic definition of justice? The answer is obvious, and no amount of clever words can explain away the racism that is so clearly evident in the absence of black power in the Catholic Church.

Why is there no clearly identifiable black theological tradition in the Catholic Church? Why are there no prominent black Catholic theologians or other scholars in religion similar to Howard Thurman, Benjamin Mays, George Kelsey, Martin Luther King, Jr., C. Eric Lincoln, and Gayraud S. Wilmore? Why are there no prominent blacks among the Latin American theologians of liberation, especially since there are more than forty million blacks in Brazil alone and nearly seventy million in all of South America? What are the factors that retard black theological development in the Catholic Church?

Of course, I do not know the answers to all these questions and do not wish to give a quick, simplistic response to them. But they are worth serious reflection and should be critically engaged by Catholic theologians and others in the Church who are concerned about its mission today. I wish only to give brief comment on some of the issues that are raised by these questions.

Unfortunately, the Catholic Church is not what it claims to be: it is not a truly *universal* church, seeking to be accountable to the whole of humanity. It is a white *European* church, almost exclusively defined by issues and problems arising from that history and culture. In order for persons of African and other non-European descent to be serious Catholics, they are virtually required to cut their relationship with their community. While this is also true of blacks in white Protestant denominations, the problem is much more serious for blacks in the Catholic Church. Being black in the Catholic Church is, at best, secondary in defining the faith or, at worst, a contradiction. Although the Catholic Church tolerates black people, and sometimes encourages their liturgical participation, the black experience is not and has never been regarded as essential to the life and work of the church. Black is not universal! Only white is—at least by implication. Black Catholics, therefore, are too much accountable to and dependent upon white, European values that are defined as Catholic dogma. European history and culture define the meaning of Scripture, tradition, and theology, and the Catholic hierarchy expects and demands that everyone, regardless of their racial identity, accept the official teachings of the church.

The white power structure in the Catholic Church is so restricting on what non-Europeans can do or say that it is almost impossible for them to do creative theology. Creative theological thinking is born out of conflict, the recognition that what *is* is *not* true, even though untruth has established itself as truth. Theology has a critical, prophetic task. It should interpret the truth of the gospel for the times in which we live so that it has continuity with the past but also challenges and exposes the present contradictions, thereby empowering the oppressed to make a new future for themselves. It was Karl Barth's concern for interpreting the truth of the gospel for the crisis situation of Europe that convinced him that one should do theology with the Bible in one hand and the newspaper in the other.

A more important example of the relationship between historical events and doing theology is found among liberation theologians in Asia, Africa, and Latin America. Without colonialism, imperialism, and the great gap between the poor masses and the rich elite, liberation theology, with its current emphasis on God's solidarity with the struggles of the poor for freedom, would not exist. All theologies are created in response to a conflict between what *is* in the church and the society and what *ought to be*. They are either seeking to conserve the status quo from supposed heretical challenges or seeking to expose and overthrow what purports to be the truth but in fact is untruth.

Ludwig Feuerbach was right: "Suffering precedes thinking." As every student of theology knows, the early christological formulations were created in the midst of conflicting claims about Jesus Christ. The same is true for every dogma that churches regard as essential for the definition of the Christian faith. Whether one speaks of the Protestant Reformation or of black church separatism, creative theological insight inevitably arises from the refusal of persons to accept what they regard as a contradiction of the faith. People who experience no conflict do not think theologically. They simply repeat what others have said. For perceptive theologians, what appears is not always real. Perceptions of reality must be tested by critically evaluating them in the light of human experience.

The evaluation of what purports to be real in the light of human experience is important for theology, because it is *people* who do theology and *not* God. As long as theology is made by human beings, it will be influenced by their history, culture, and interests. This may sound like an elementary point, but when blacks read the textbooks on Catholic theology, we find that they are written as if the white experience is universal. The experiences of blacks and other people of color are made invisible in Catholic theology. When questioned about this conspicuous omission, white Catholic intellectuals, like many Protestants, often say that theology has to do with God and not with the history and culture of ethnic minorities. They steadfastly refuse to acknowledge that their theology is a product of the white ethnic values of Europe and America.

The acknowledgment of the social character of theological reflection is important not only because theologians are human beings but also because of the incarnation of God in Jesus Christ. By becoming human in Jesus, God took humanity seriously. We are all created in God's image—black, red, brown, and white people, even though whites often act as if their history and culture exhaust the content of humanity's meaning.

Because Europeans are extremely rigid in their definition of theology, all Third World peoples have been theologically stifled by an inordinate dependence upon others to do their thinking about God for them. How is it possible for Third World Christians to develop a creative theology if they are dependent upon the approval of those who are responsible for their oppression? How is it possible for Third World peoples to develop a liberating theology if their history and culture are regarded as inappropriate sources for doing theology?

It was because of the extreme exploitation of the black community, especially in the urban ghettos, that a few radical black preachers and activists were forced to develop a black theology during the 1960s. Although white theologians, Catholic and Protestant, ignored and sometimes condemned the rise of the black struggle for justice, black preachers' commitment to that struggle necessitated their rereading of the Bible so that they could retain their Christian identity and also their commitment to freedom. This was the theological contradiction that gave birth to black theology.

A similar theological contradiction encouraged the development of feminist and other liberation theologies among the victims of North America. There are also Third World liberation theologies in Africa, Asia, and Latin America. Although each form of liberation theology has its own unique focus and concern, they agree that the struggle for justice is the paramount issue for today's church. They also formed an organization called the Ecumenical Association of Third World Theologians (EATWOT) for the purpose of developing ways in which they can mutually support each other in the struggle for justice. A similar theological coalition occurred among U.S. minorities in an organization called the Theology in the Americas (TIA), giving birth to dialogues in their respective communities. Third World Christians have begun to realize the need for solidarity and support for each other in their struggles for liberation.

Like my Third World sisters and brothers, I believe that the time has come for the victims of injustice to do their own thinking in theology. As Gustavo Gutiérrez says, "Even the poor have the right to think. The right to think is a corollary of the right to be, and to assert the right to think is only to assert the right to exist."

By ignoring the theological and political reflections of blacks and other minorities in their churches and other contexts, white Catholics are saying that black and other poor people cannot think. That is why most whites ignore black theology.

We blacks will consider what white Catholics say about theology and justice as seriously as they consider what we say about those subjects. If whites ignore us, we will *not* ignore them. But we blacks cannot accept what they say about justice when they have not even consulted the black experience in the development of their definition. Indeed, we must remain suspicious of any theological talk that does not enhance the chances for life of poor people in their fight for justice. Let us hope that blacks, whites, Hispanics, Native Americans, Asians, women, and the poor of all groups throughout the world can begin to develop ideas of justice and of God that are accountable to the experience of liberation in our histories and cultures. Only then can we become the beloved community about which Martin Luther King, Jr., spoke so eloquently and for which Jesus Christ gave his life.

Violence and Vengeance:
A Perspective

WHEN I WAS ASKED TO SPEAK ON THE SUBJECT OF "VIOLENCE AND vengeance" by the National Inter-religious Task Force on Criminal Justice, I hesitated and discussed my concerns with the organizers of this conference before accepting the invitation. The reasons are many and obvious. Violence is a very complex issue, global in its manifestations and difficult to define. There is no way, with my limited competence and the time available for preparation, I can address the legitimate concerns of all who have been victimized by it and who are actively engaged in its control and elimination. There is the violence between races, vividly revealed in the long history of the persecution of Jews, the oppression of blacks and other minorities by whites in the Americas, and the colonial and neocolonial exploitation of Africa, Asia, and Latin America by Europe, the United States, and the Soviet Union. There is the violence that men inflict upon women— perhaps the oldest and definitely one of the least recognized forms of human exploitation. Sexist violence is dramatically revealed in the phenomenon of rape. But it is found wherever men think and act as if they have the right to determine the place of women in the church, home, and society. There is also the violence of the rich against the poor, painfully visible in the relations between classes in many societies and also in the relations between nations. Violence is found on the streets of the cities, in the home and the school, between parents and children, and among the youth who prey upon the elderly. There is nowhere we can go without being confronted with blatant manifestations of violence.

With the manifestations of violence being so widespread and

This essay is a revised version of an address prepared for the National Conference on the Religious Community's Roles in Breaking the Cycle of Violence and Vengeance, held in Indianapolis, Indiana, 2-5 November 1984.

its definition elusive, how can I, a black Christian theologian, speak for so many victims—most of whom are neither black nor Christian and not even interested in theology? If I were speaking to *only* black Christians, my task would not be nearly as difficult. For there is a common history of struggle against violence in the black community and a faith that sustains us in our struggle, enabling us to transcend our differences, and thereby making genuine dialogue possible. But when people's histories and affirmations of faith are markedly different and often contradictory, communication across race, class, and gender lines is nearly impossible, even though they may be citizens of the same country and adherents of the same religion.

But despite all the reasons which encourage our silence, the gravity of the problem of violence in this society and the world and the urgency of the need to find ways to control and eliminate its most destructive manifestations require all responsible persons to face this issue squarely, speaking forcefully and frankly. No one person, group, or nation can eliminate violence alone. All persons concerned about the survival and health of human beings must join together to renounce violence or it will devour us all. I have come here today because I believe that the Christian church has a special responsibility to create a world free of violence.

We cannot, however, create a world without violence if we do not analyze carefully its causes, fight untiringly for justice and peace, and identify the persons and socio-political structures most responsible for human misery. Pious generalities, so typical of church rhetoric, do more harm than good, because they keep us from locating the root causes of violence and from identifying the real enemies of freedom.

In my address, I want to offer some reflections which I hope will not only motivate us to probe more deeply the causes and manifestations of violence and vengeance, but will also provide some guidelines for the church in its struggle to create a world of justice and peace for all.

Some Reflections on Violence and Vengeance

Violence is commonly defined as "physical force exerted for the purpose of violating, damaging, or abusing." War is the most obvious example of violence defined in this way. That was why

Macaulay, the English historian and statesman, said, "The essence of war is violence."

The United States has been involved in many acts of violence: the Revolutionary War that gave birth to the nation; the War of 1812; the many wars with Native Americans; the Mexican-American War; the Civil War; the invasions of the Philippines and Puerto Rico; World Wars I and II; the Korean and Vietnam Wars; the invasions of Cuba, the Dominican Republic, and Grenada; and currently the wars in the Middle East, Central America, and in many other places where the highly sophisticated intelligence of the CIA and the military are being used.

President Reagan has spoken of the United States' involvement in the affairs of other nations as "covert actions" and "peacemaking missions," and he has said that they are "making the world safe for democracy and freedom." Others, however, view the President's actions in a different light. In a *New York Times* editorial, Tad Szulc, a writer for *Foreign Affairs,* referred to Reagan's policy as "making the world 'safe' for hypocrisy."[1] His point was to demonstrate the absence of any correlation between a genuine concern for democracy and Reagan's order that the U.S. military invade Grenada. What President Reagan calls "a nation with global responsibility" is interpreted by others as a militaristic nation defending the corporate capital of the rich First World countries at the expense of Third World countries with great numbers of poor people.

I am sure that many Third World Christians will be pleased to know that the churches in the United States have come together in a national conference because of their concern about the religious community's role in breaking the cycle of violence and vengeance. But for others, our meeting will have a touch of irony, because our churches have often been conspicuously silent as U.S. and European armies plundered Third World countries with violence—especially in the forms of slavery, colonialism, and economic exploitation. Presently, no nation has America's resources for military destruction; and every nation of the Third World knows how quickly retaliation is meted out at the slightest challenge to its self-proclaimed right to police the world for capitalist interests. Of course, the U.S. State Department has nice phrases to describe its clandestine and violent activities: "preven-

1. Szulc, *New York Times,* 28 October 1983, p. A27.

tive measures" instead of revenge, "covert actions" in lieu of ter-
rorism. But such niceties of language do not change the consequences of such actions for the dead or the injured.

When we combine the violent actions of the United States
military with those of other countries, particularly the Soviet
Union, the enormity of violence is staggering. It is a disease of the
modern world. Indeed, as Hannah Arendt has said, the "tech-
nological development of the instruments of violence has now
reached the point where no political goal could conceivabley cor-
respond to their destructive potential or justify their actual use in
armed conflict."[2] With President Reagan's determined commitment of research for the Star Wars project (the dream of exotic
space-based battle stations designed to knock out Soviet missiles
and warheads) and with Russian leaders' determination to coun-
ter with equal means of nuclear destruction, the possibility of the
ultimate holocaust extinguishing the human species is a realistic
fear of the terrible times in which we live today.

People have seldom allowed any feelings of moral restraint to
serve as a guide to their political judgment and military actions. Is
it reasonable to expect people to possess weapons of destruction
and not use them in acts of war? We know that if Hitler had had
the Bomb, he would have used it, as the U.S. did against Japan,
even in a situation that many say was not necessary for victory.
And there is every reason to believe that the Reagan administration and Soviet leaders would do the same if they perceived their
nation to be in danger of being defeated militarily.

The gravity of our situation requires not only that we pray
more reverently for justice and peace, using all the resources our
faith has given us, but also that we develop more sophisticated
analyses of how we got into this mess and of what we must do to
get out of it. I believe that we must continue our search for answers to the problem of violence, refusing to cooperate with its
perpetrators, and rejecting the idea that there is nothing we can
do about it.

It is not only violence between nations that threatens human
survival; it is also violence between individuals and between citizens and the law enforcement officers in their community. Do-
mestic violence is dramatically portrayed daily over the local and
national TV news and in the newspapers. The breakdown of
human values is so pervasive that it is no longer safe to walk the

2. Arendt, *On Violence* (New York: Harcourt, Brace & World, 1969), p. 3.

streets of our cities at night and in some places during the day. Men are raping women, youths are terrorizing the elderly, and the Ku Klux Klan and Neo-Nazi groups are once again parading through the streets, spreading their hatred of blacks, Jews, Catholics, and other religious and racial minorities. All kinds of hate groups are emerging proclaiming their right to exist, even if their existence means nonexistence for their victims. The ever-present reality of violence engulfs our world to the degree that we never know what to expect from the next person we meet. We do not know whether he or she is going to attack us or greet us in friendship and love.

The violence in the streets has created war zone areas, and much of it is due to the violent behavior of the police, the persons responsible for keeping the peace. Blacks, Hispanics, and poor men, women, and children of every race are constantly harrassed, beaten, and shot by white policemen in New Orleans, Philadelphia, New York, Chicago, and practically every city in the United States where people seek to assert their right to be treated as human beings. The jails, prisons, and other detention centers are terrible reminders that there can be no peace without justice, even though many whites and other middle-class people often act like there is no relationship between the two. There can be no reconciliation without liberation, another fact that some people conveniently forget. Physical violence between blacks and whites, men and women, Jews and Gentiles, rich and poor will not cease until those who control the instruments of violence lay down their arms with the intention of treating every person as a human being. Talk about nonviolence as a black response to white brutality is nothing but hyprocrisy, since whites have never been and are not now nonviolent in their relations with blacks and others they perceive as a threat to their well-being.

The fact that I point out the hypocrisy of whites with regard to violence does not mean that I would counsel blacks to be violent toward whites. Returning violence for violence must be completely rejected as an inappropriate strategy for black liberation in the United States. As Martin Luther King, Jr., often pointed out, "As a way of achieving racial justice . . . violence is not the way." It is "both impractical and immoral."[3]

Although I completely reject violence as a method for achiev-

---

3. King, in *"I Have a Dream": The Quotations of Martin Luther King, Jr.*, ed. Lotte Hoakins (New York: Grosset & Dunlap, 1968), p. 148.

ing justice in the United States, this does not mean that I am prepared to advise blacks to listen to white Christians and other moralists as they urge the victims to be nonviolent and passive in the face of the violence of whites. The people who brought blacks to this continent on slave ships and auctioned them off to the highest bidder, in the name of God and country, are in no moral position to request nonviolence from their victims. It is an unseemly request, completely out of place; and I am nonplused by the fact that it should be necessary to remind whites of it. No whites should tell blacks or any of their other victims that they should be nonviolent in response to white violence. Whites should take their own advice and incorporate it into their own behavior.

If whites had practiced nonviolence or even a measure of physical restraint, they would not have enslaved Africans or exploited other racial minorities. If whites had practiced nonviolence, the United States and Russia would not be approaching the danger of a nuclear holocaust.

It is most revealing that nuclear weapons were developed first in a nation that defined itself as Christian. What does that say about the morality of the churches of such a nation when they said so little in protest against it? The Bomb was tested on Hiroshima and Nagasaki with little complaint from the churches. Today the Bomb that "civilized" whites created has come back to devour its creators as well as the rest of us. Malcolm X was more prophetic than whites care to admit: "the chickens are coming home to roost."

Blacks and other victims of white violence are not surprised by the nuclear nightmare that has been created. That is why blacks, unfortunately, are seldom found in the crowds protesting nuclear arms. We have lived with white violence for nearly four hundred years, faced slave ships, auction blocks, lynchings, ghettos, inadequate education and medical care, indecent housing, chronic unemployment, and constant police brutality. When physical survival is a daily task in which the odds are against you, because the nation in which you are a citizen has defined you as the enemy, there is little motivation to protest against a nuclear crisis that your enemies have created, especially when the people protesting look like your oppressors and do so little to connect justice with peace issues.

When physical violence is related to the violence against one's

personhood, the enormity of the problem of violence is staggering and the possibility of eliminating it or bringing it under control seems remote. Injustice in any form is violence, and it comes
in many manifestations. There is not only violence *in* the slum but
there is also the violence *of* the slum. There is not only the violence in the school but the violence of the school—graduating
blacks, Hispanics, and other poor children who cannot read or
write and are thus incapable of functioning creatively in the society. There is not only the violence in the prisons and jails but also
the violence of the prisons and jails. It is hard to take white Christians' appeals for nonviolence seriously when they are so selective
about their definition of violence. As Malcolm X said,

> By violence they only mean when a black [person] protects
> himself [or herself] against the attacks of a white [person]. This
> is what they mean by violence. They don't mean what you
> mean. Because they don't even use the word violence until
> someone gives the impression that *you're* about to explode.
> When it comes time for . . . black [people] to explode they call it
> violence. But white people can be exploding against black peo-
> ple all day long, and it's never called violence. I even have [had
> some blacks] come to me and ask me, am I for violence? I'm the
> victim of violence. But you've been so victimized by it that you
> can't recognize it for what it is today.[4]

When I say that injustice is violence, I mean that the "slum
environment, the structure of the slum itself, works violence
against those who live within it, even if they never experience the
physical harm so often attendant on slum dwelling."[5] Aristotle
defined justice as giving every person his or her due. The former
president of Union Seminary and one of the most prominent
theologians in the United States, John Bennett, has given an even
more insightful definition for our time: justice is "giving every
child his [or her] due."[6] As Robert M. Brown says, "When society
is so organized that any child is deprived of those things he [or
she] is entitled to have (food, clothing, education, for example),
that society is unjust and is engaging in violence against that

4. Malcolm X, in *By Any Means Necessary*, ed. George Breitman (New York:
Pathfinder, 1970), p. 176.
5. Robert M. Brown, *Religion and Violence* (Philadelphia: Westminster Press,
1973), pp. 35-36.
6. Bennet, cited by Brown, in *Religion and Violence*, p. 9.

child."[7] Unfortunately, when many middle-class people speak of violence they seldom identify it with the violation of personhood, because their personhood is seldom violated. But for those who are the victims, the violence against one's person is real even though it may be hidden from the view of those who are not its victims. Violence against personhood transforms a person into a thing to be used for the interests of another. It is institutional, structural violence. The violation of one's personhood means that who you are and what your people's history and culture stand for count as nothing in the eyes of the rulers in the society. For blacks to be successful in the white world, they are often forced to integrate, identifying with the values responsible for black oppression. That was why Malcolm X said that "the worst crime the white man has committed has been to teach us to hate ourselves."

Middle-class professionals have the luxury of discussing violence in the peaceful surroundings of a well-protected, comfortable hotel. We do not have to worry about violent persons disrupting our meeting, because there are law enforcement officers armed and ready to come to our aid. But there are many poor persons in this society and the world who have no one to protect them from those who would violate their humanity. In fact, the same police officers who protect whites violate the humanity of blacks and other minorities. Therefore if we expect the poor to take us seriously, we must make the unequitable way in which laws are enacted and enforced the prime manifestation of violence in this society. We should not allow our middle-class status to blind us to violence embedded in social, economic, and political structures. Indeed, many of the violent acts the poor commit in our cities and prisons are due to the injustice with which they have to cope. When people have no jobs in which to support themselves or their families, what are they to do, especially in a society of plenty whose expenditures for armaments of destruction are approaching $300 billion yearly? Must the poor starve as our government makes more bombs that could destroy the whole of human life? Unless we are willing to change places with the poor, or at least fight for their right to bread and life, we have no right to condemn those who commit acts of violence as a last resort for survival.

7. Brown, *Religion and Violence*, p. 9.

The problem of violence is enhanced because the victims often respond with vengeance, a vindictiveness that seeks to give the perpetrators of violence some of their own medicine. When the poor of the world analyze the structures of injustice and begin to realize that their poverty is calculated and directly traceable to the actions of the rich, they often respond with violent acts of revenge. Some acts of revenge were committed during the unrest of the 1960s as Black Power advocates urged black people to defend their right to life, liberty, and the pursuit of happiness. They took their cue from the Declaration of Independence, from the Constitution, and from many white Christians who have always exacted from their enemies far more punishment than any crime against them would warrant by any objective standard of morality.

Although I understand why many black victims of white violence develop deep feelings of hate and revenge toward whites, I cannot support any act of vengeance. I must reject it not only because I am a Christian, and thus believe that vengeance belongs to God alone; I must repudiate it because persons who hate are themselves destroyed by the hate and rendered unfit as creative bearers of the new social order. Revenge may be understandable in view of the enormity of the violence that oppressors commit against their victims, but it cannot be condoned, because it destroys the humanity we claim to be defending. Revolutions should be made because of love and not hate. As Che Guevara said, "A revolutionary act is an act of love"—love not only for the victims but for the victimizer as well. That was why Camilo Torres said, "Revolutionary action is a Christian, a priestly struggle."

Because a true revolutionary is a lover of humanity, we must be careful how we define vengeance. For "Christian" oppressors, any act by the oppressed is almost always interpreted as vengeance. Oppressors like their victims to be passive, and religion is often used as an effective instrument to keep the poor submissive while oppressors rob them of their humanity. White Christians are well-known for their counsel to blacks in this regard, using carefully selected Bible texts and sayings of black leaders as evidence that blacks should not defend themselves against white brutality.

Vengeance should not be confused with self-defense. Vengeance is inflicting punishment for the purpose of revenge, a retaliatory act of violence in payment for an injury committed.

Self-defense is "defense of oneself when physically attacked." Black victims of racially motivated violence have the right, morally and legally, to protect themselves against the brutality of white hate groups who assume that merely because they are white they have the right to violate black humanity.

No amount of twisted Christian rhetoric should be allowed to confuse self-defense with vengeance. Self-defense is nothing but the defense of one's right to exist with dignity. No one expressed this point for the black community more forcefully than Malcolm X: "Respect me, or put me to death. But when you start to put me to death, we're both going to die together."[8]

To black and white critics who incorrectly labeled Malcolm a promoter of violence and hate, he replied,

> This is not violence. This is intelligence. As soon as you [blacks] start even thinking like that, they say you're advocating violence. No, you're advocating intelligence. Didn't you hear Lyndon B. Johnson last week when he said that they'll go to war in a minute to protect their life, liberty, and pursuit of happiness? Did they say LBJ was violent? No, they said he was a good president. Well, let's you and I be good presidents.[9]

Malcolm rejected violence because he really wanted peace. But he wanted it with justice. Order without justice is nothing but legalized violence.

> It's time for you and me now to let the world know how peaceful we are, how well-meaning we are, how law-abiding we wish to be. But at the same time we have to let the same world know we'll blow their world skyhigh if we're not respected and recognized and treated the same as other human beings are treated. If you won't tell them that, you need to just get off the planet. You shouldn't even be around in the company of people. No, in fact, you should be too ashamed to be seen out in public because you're not a [person], you're less than a [person], subhuman.[10]

Words of Advice for Churches

As can be clearly seen in what I have already said, my perspective on violence and vengeance has been strongly influenced by

---

8. Malcolm X, *By Any Means Necessary*, p. 86.
9. Malcolm X, *By Any Means Necessary*, p. 87.
10. Malcolm X, *By Any Means Necessary*, p. 87.

the life and thought of Malcolm X. His influence makes black identity and self-defense important in my analysis. He forces me to think from the vantage point of the victims, refusing to accept the logic of oppressors as the appropriate way to think about justice, peace, and violence. "Don't let anybody who is oppressing us ever lay the ground rules," he said. "Don't go by their game, don't play the game by their rules. Let them know now that this is a new game, and we've got some new rules, and these rules mean anything goes."[11] Although whites portrayed Malcolm as a champion of hatred and violence, nothing could have been further from his intentions. He merely liberated the minds of many blacks, destroying their self-hate by advocating respect for and love of blackness. When blacks heard Malcolm, many were empowered for the first time to stand up like human beings and claim their dignity.

It was Malcolm's challenge to the Christian Church that motivated me to think deeper about the relationship between the black experience and the Christian faith. His logic was so persuasive: "I believe in a religion that believes in freedom. Any time I have to accept a religion that won't let me fight a battle for my people, I say to hell with that religion."[12] Does Christianity believe in black freedom and will it let me fight for it? Wrestling with that question forced me to become a theologian of black liberation. It was clear to me then and now that if the answer had been negative, I could not be a Christian.

The life and thought of Martin Luther King, Jr., is as important as that of Malcolm X for my theological perspective. King demonstrated that fighting for the freedom of the "least of these" is not an option that Christians can take or leave depending upon their moral disposition. Solidarity with the poor and the wretched is a necessity that arises from the essence of Christian obedience.

God created us as one humanity, made for each other because we are God's children. But the condition of the poor is a blatant denial of our oneness. Freedom has to be for everybody or it can be for nobody. King articulated the interconnectedness of life when he said that

> All life is interrelated. . . . Injustice anywhere is a threat to justice everywhere. . . . Whatever affects one directly affects all indirectly. I can never be what I ought to be until you are what

11. Malcolm X, *By Any Means Necessary,* p. 155.
12. Malcolm X, *By Any Means Necessary,* p. 140.

you ought to be, and you can never be what you ought to be until I am what I ought to be. This is the interrelated structure of reality.[13]

It is our common humanity, a gift from God affirmed in our struggle for justice and peace, that binds us together into one community. I believe, like King, that blacks and whites, men and women, young and old, Christians and non-Christians—all human beings interested in peace and justice and the elimination of violence and vengeance—must join together to create a just and sane society. We must break the cycle of violence and vengeance, or else hatred combined with the nuclear implements of violence will destroy us all.

Because of the escalation and pervasiveness of violence in the world today, it is imperative that Christians make clear where they stand and why. As a black theologian, I offer some words of advice to white, black, and other middle-class Christians.

1. Do not tell the victims of violence (i.e., the poor and the wretched of the earth) to be nonviolent and passive unless you are willing to share their lot and experience the depth of their suffering and deprivation. Middle-class white and black Christians, whose daily experience of injustice is minimal when compared to that of the poor, are in no moral position to tell poor people what to do about injustice. We earn our right to speak for the poor when we share their lot. When we speak in a self-righteous tone about the values of nonviolence for the poor and yet support the violence of the U.S. government in the Third World and the violence of the police in black and poor communities, we expose clearly the hypocrisy of much of what passes for Christianity in this society. As Jean Genet said,

> It is evident that recommending nonviolence to blacks is an effort to retain the Christian vocabulary which has kept them imprisoned in passivity for so long. However Christian the whites are, they don't feel guilty about using guns: that is violence. Asking blacks in America to be nonviolent means that whites are demanding a Christian virtue which they themselves do not possess. That means that whites are once again trying to dupe the blacks.[14]

13. King, in *"I Have a Dream,"* pp. 79, 80.
14. Genet, "Here and Now for Bobby Seale," *Ramparts* (June 1970, p. 31), cited by Brown in *Religion and Violence*, p. x.

2. If you believe, as I do, that nonviolence has an important place in the Christian ethic, then you should be able to see that it is necessary for the churches to embody it by bearing the cross of the poor and taking their pain and suffering upon themselves as Jesus did during his ministry and in death. We will earn the right to speak of Jesus' reconciliation and of King's beloved community when we embody a similar ministry. We must practice what we preach by becoming genuine friends of the poor, making their lot the lot of the churches. This is the only way that the message of nonviolence will have any credibility in our time.

3. We must join forces with the victims who are struggling for justice here and abroad. Fighting for justice is the only way to eliminate violence and vengeance and to establish peace. There can be no peace without justice, and there can be no justice apart from the creative input of the history and culture of the victims. As we struggle for justice and peace, it is necessary to remember that freedom is not free; it must be taken from those who would claim more for themselves than they ought. As Frederick Douglass put it,

> If there is no struggle, there is no progress. Those who profess to favor freedom, and yet depreciate agitation, are [persons] who want crops without plowing up the ground. They want rain without thunder and lightning. . . . This struggle may be a moral one; or it may be a physical one; or it may be both moral and physical; but there must be a struggle.[15]

Even Gunnar Myrdal, the Swedish social scientist, a liberal who is not given to careless revolutionary rhetoric, has made the same point:

> No upper class has ever stepped down voluntarily to equality with the lower class, and as a simple consequence of moral conviction given up their privileges and opened entrance to their monopolies. To be induced to do so, the rich and privileged must sense that demands are raised and forcefully pressed, and that power becomes assembled behind them.[16]

There is no way that one can be impartial in the struggle between the rich and the poor. As Reinhold Niebuhr noted, "Neu-

---

15. Douglass, cited by me in *Black Theology and Black Power*, p. 3.
16. Myrdal, *Beyond the Welfare State: Economic Planning and Its International Implications* (1960; Westport, Conn.: Greenwood Books, 1982), p. 227. Cited by R. M. Brown in *Religion and Violence*, p. 66.

trality in a social struggle between entrenched and advancing social classes means alliance with the entrenched position. In the social struggle we are either on the side of privilege or need."[17] The crucial issue for the Christian is not violence or nonviolence but rather whose side we are on in the struggle for freedom. I firmly believe the gospel demands that we take sides with the victims of injustice and not with the oppressors. There is no third way, no neutral position for the Christian.

Throughout their long history, Western churches have often taken the side of the powerful rather than the weak. That is why the fighters for justice are often anti-Christian or at least suspicious of the churches. Religion has served as an opiate, a tranquilizer to make the poor quiet and content with their poverty. If we expect to create an image of the church defending freedom and justice for all persons, then the burden is upon us to show that we are willing to suffer with the poor nonviolently and not simply advise them to do what we would not do were we in their situation.

In a time when the United States and Russia are engaged in a nuclear arms race, the churches must insist that this madness be stopped. It is not the violence of the poor that has created the risk of a nuclear holocaust; that threat is due to the insanity of "civilized" white men. The Third World poor do not understand why many advantaged Christians of the United States actively support the violence of their government in Central America but express horror when the poor resist injustice with physical force. What is it that makes the violent acts of our government in Central America acceptable to the "Christian" conscience and the actions of Latin American people who resist the U.S. military unacceptable terrorists acts?

To break the cycle of violence, Christians ought to assert an unqualified solidarity with those who are the victims of injustice. As long as we allow the enemies of the Christian gospel to enhance their privilege and exploit the poor, we will simply add more fuel to the fires of violence and vengeance, causing injustice to become even more entrenched.

It is not often that I approvingly quote a president of the United States, but a statement by John F. Kennedy is one of the important exceptions: "Those who make peaceful revolution im-

17. Niebuhr, cited by Brown in *Religion and Violence*, p. 73.

possible make violent revolution inevitable." Let us hope that we will leave this place with a much deeper commitment to stand with the poor—not because we feel sorry for them but because they are our brothers and sisters, who embody within their personhood our own humanity.

4. To overcome violence and vengeance, it is necessary to organize, because there is no way to defeat evil without a carefully defined plan of action. Action without a thoughtfully worked out strategy is aimless activity which actually supports the injustice we are reacting against. We must develop nonviolent direct action and civil disobedience tactics that will be disruptive enough to force those in power to listen to us and respond meaningfully to our demands of justice for the poor.

Organizing for the establishment of justice must be global in its perspective. There is a close correlation between what our government does to the poor at home and what it does abroad, especially in the Third World. Our resistance against the violent actions of the U.S. government in Central America and its economic support of apartheid in South Africa and other oppressive Third World nations must be so strong that the Reagan administration will be forced to change its foreign policy.

A similar act of resistance must take place at home on behalf of the poor who are daily victimized by the police and a grossly unjust socio-economic structure. In addition to holding the police accountable to the people in whose community they are assigned to serve, there is also the need to begin the task of remaking the entire political economy in the United States. As King said to the Southern Christian Leadership Conference staff in 1967,

> Now, when we see that there must be a radical redistribution of economic and political power, then we see that for the last twelve years we have been in a reform movement. We were seeking to reform certain conditions in the house of our nation because the nation wasn't living up to the very rules of the house that it had prescribed in the Constitution. That after Selma and the Voting Rights Bill, we moved into a new era, which must be an era of revolution. I think we must see that great distinction between a reform movement and a revolutionary movement.
>
> Now we are called upon to raise some questions about the house itself. Now we are in a situation where we must ask the

house to change its rules, because the rules themselves don't go far enough. In short, we have moved into an era where we are called upon to raise certain basic questions about the whole society. We are still called upon to give aid to the beggar who finds himself in misery and agony on life's highway. But one day, we must ask the question of whether an edifice which produces beggars must not be restructured.[18]

This quotation is an example of the radical change that was occurring in King's thinking after Selma and the passage of the Voting Rights Bill in 1965. He realized that the capitalist economy of the United States rewards the rich at the expense of the poor and that it had to be completely restructured. In private circles, he even spoke of the new economic structure in radical terms, using the words "Marxism" and "socialism" to describe it.[19] This is not the King of the 1963 March on Washington who proclaimed his optimistic dream of justice, peace, and integration. Neither is it the King that the U.S. Congress honored with a national holiday. The "1963 King" is too optimistic about integration, and the "Congress King" is too respectable and plastic. Congress was trying to domesticate King by transforming his genuinely prophetic voice into the "voice of America."

Because King is in danger of being domesticated, it is necessary to place Malcolm X by his side as a corrective and a reminder that both preached the same message—the liberation of the poor from the violence of the rich. It is harder to domesticate Malcolm,

---

18. King, "To Charter Our Course for the Future," a thirty-five-page unpublished transcript of King's remarks to an SCLC staff retreat held in Frogmore, South Carolina, 29-31 May 1967, pp. 8-9.

19. In recent years, there has been some discussion regarding the rapid growth of King's radicalism, which began around the fall of 1965. The most important study in this regard is the research of David J. Garrow. See his study *The FBI and Martin Luther King, Jr.: From "Solo" to Memphis* (New York: Norton, 1981), especially chap. 6. See also his essay "From Reformer to Revolutionary," published by Democratic Socialists of America. His book *Bearing the Cross: Martin Luther King, Jr., and the Southern Christian Leadership Conference, 1955-1968* (Garden City, N.Y.: Doubleday, 1986) provides more data regarding King's radicalism. See also Adam Fairclough's article "Was Martin Luther King a Marxist?" in *History Workshop Journal*, a journal of socialist and feminist historians, Spring 1983. I know of no one who would claim that King was a Marxist-Leninist. But there are many persons who say that he made radical claims among friends in private conversations about the political economy, things he would not say in public.

because he spoke the truth in clear, forceful, and uncompromising language. Regarding capitalism, he said,

> It is impossible for capitalism to survive, primarily because the system of capitalism needs some blood to suck. Capitalism used to be like an eagle, but now it's more like a vulture. It used to be strong enough to go and suck anybody's blood whether they were strong or not. But now it has become more cowardly, like the vulture, and it can only suck the blood of the helpless. As the nations of the world free themselves, then capitalism has less victims, less to suck, and it becomes weaker and weaker. It's only a matter of time in my opinion before it will collapse completely.[20]

5. We must be careful not to allow the perpetrators of official violence to create despair in our struggle for justice and peace. They will try to make us think that there is nothing we can do to end the nuclear arms race and the violence of the CIA throughout the world. But I contend that we can end it, because there can be no democratic government without the consent of the people—that is, without our consent. We must let the powers that be know that they do not have our consent to commit violence here or abroad.

In our opposition, we must not be too selective regarding the forms of violence that we oppose. Racism, sexism, classism, militarism, neocolonialism, ageism, and all other kinds of human violation must be resisted. Blacks must be careful not to limit their struggle against violence to racism. Women must not limit their concern to sexist violence. The same is true of others. This point is important, because oppressions are interconnected. The values of the racists and sexists are similar and are often found in the same persons and structures. To fight one form of violence effectively is to see it in relationship with other forms.

6. As we struggle against the "principalities and powers," let us remember that we do not struggle alone. The God of Abraham and Sarah, of Moses and Ruth, of Jesus and Mary is present with us. It is God's presence with the poor that empowers them with courage and strength to fight for freedom even though the odds against them are great.

The black community of faith provided the occasion for my

20. Malcolm X, *By Any Means Necessary*, pp. 165-66.

existential encounter with the God of Jesus, the One who establishes justice and heals the wounds of the oppressed. It was at Macedonia African Methodist Episcopal Church of Bearden that I first learned that "Jesus does not leave the little ones alone in trouble." The people of Macedonia contended that "he is strength where there is weakness," "joy where there is sorrow," and "food when souls are hungry." "Jesus," they said, "is the name!" They also said, "he is mighty as a mountain," "broader than the river," and "deeper than the ocean." They referred to Jesus as "the great Son of Jehovah," "the mighty Prince of Peace," and "the everlasting Savior."

> He is water when we're thirsty,
> He's a ruler in high places,
> He's a pillar I can lean on,
> Jesus is the name!

In the black community, God and Jesus stand for that reality of a divine presence who sustains the people in their struggle and gives them courage and strength to fight back. Divine presence in the struggle, however, is not a replacement for human initiative. Rather, God empowers the poor so they will know that their fight is not in vain. Black religion is defined by *hope*, not despair. Although black Christians encounter trials and tribulations, they still refuse to allow despair to define their existence. They contend that "there is a balm in Gilead" who gives hope to the discouraged and revives them for struggle. Black Christians do not deny that the struggle is hard and the road to freedom is rough. But they claim that God is hope for the despairing, joy for the sorrowful. With Jesus *standing* with them, they believe that nothing can separate them from freedom. That is why they sing:

> When the storms of life are raging,
> Stand by me;
> When the storms of life are raging,
> Stand by me.
> When the world is tossing me,
> Like a ship upon the sea;
> Thou who rulest the wind and water,
> Stand by me.
>
> In the midst of tribulation,
> Stand by me;

In the midst of tribulation,
Stand by me.
When the hosts of hell assail,
And my strength begins to fail,
Thou who never lost a battle,
Stand by me.

PART II

Black Churches, Ecumenism, and the Liberation Struggle

THE IDEA OF A BLACK THEOLOGY OF LIBERATION WAS NOT CREATED in the seminary or university. It emerged out of black churches which have been involved in the black liberation struggle from the time of their origin to the present day. The essays in Part II analyze the strengths and weaknesses of the historical and theological self-understanding of black churches, particularly as defined by the multifaceted roles which they have played in the struggles of African-Americans for justice in American society.

"Black Religious Thought in American History" is an analysis of the themes of liberation, justice, love, suffering, and hope in black churches from slavery to the rise of black theology in the 1960s. It was written in 1984 for the *Encyclopedia of Religion in America*.

I have never claimed an exclusive status for black churches or black theology in relation to other churches of the world, including white denominations. To be sure, I have been critical of white churches for their racism and for their support of the rich against the poor. But I have also been critical of black churches for their imitation of the white ones from which they separated. Both black and white churches are accountable to the one God who is the Creator of all. In the essay "What Is the Church?" my concern is to examine the theological and sociological aspects of the church from the perspective of its christological foundation. It was initially written for a pastor's conference on the church at Emory University (Atlanta, 1980) and later rewritten for a conference on "Jesus and Justice" held at Philander Smith College (Little Rock, 1985).

The separation of black and white churches in worship and other aspects of their life is a scandal, because each claims that

81

Jesus Christ is Lord. In the essay "Black Worship: A Historical-Theological Interpretation" I attempt to show that this separation cannot be reduced to social realities unrelated to their theological identity. To worship together as a community, persons must live together in community, and to live together as one people of God, white and black Christians must believe and act as if God has given them an identity that transcends the human barriers designed to separate them. This means that both can achieve their Christian identity only through an unqualified solidarity with the victims of oppression, seeing in their struggles of liberation God's eschatological sign to make us all one.

There is no greater scandal for black churches than their continued separation from each other, which impedes the liberation struggle in the black community. Denominationalism is a disease that makes black church people more concerned about their Baptist, African Methodist Episcopal, African Methodist Episcopal Zion, or Pentecostal identity than they are about proclaiming and living the gospel of Jesus. In the concluding essay, "Black Ecumenism and the Liberation Struggle," I attempt to show that ecumenism is not an option that we can take or leave, depending upon our ecumenical disposition. Rather, it is a necessity that arises from the nature of the gospel and from the urgent times in which we live. If black churches cannot achieve unity among themselves, how can they expect anyone to believe that they are separated from white churches *only* because of the latter's racism? Unless Christians can achieve a unity in Christ that is more important than the accidents of race, creed, and nationality, we have no right to claim that Jesus Christ is Lord.

Black Religious Thought in
American History
Part I: Origins

God is not dead,—nor is he an indifferent onlooker at what is
going on in this world. One day He will make restitution for
blood; He will call the oppressors to account. Justice may sleep,
but it never dies. The individual, race, or nation which does
wrong, which sets at defiance God's great law, especially God's
great law of love, of brotherhood, will be sure, sooner or late, to
pay the penalty. We reap as we sow. With that measure we mete,
it shall be measured to us again.

                                   The Rev. Francis J. Grimke (1902)[1]

FRANCIS J. GRIMKE'S STATEMENT IS AN APT SUMMARY OF THE MAJOR
themes in black religious thought from the late eighteenth century to the present day. Black religious thought has been primarily Christian, but strongly influenced by its African back-
ground and the struggle of black people to liberate themselves
from slavery and second-class citizenship in North America. Because it has been developed in response to the involuntary servitude of Africans and the subsequent black struggle for equality
in the United States, it has never been exclusively Christian or
primarily concerned with the explication of creeds and doctrines
as found in the dominant theologies of Europe and America.
Theology as "rational reflection" about God was foreign to the
intellectual and religious sensibilities of African slaves. Most

---

1. From *The Works of Francis J. Grimke,* ed. C. G. Woodson (Washington: Associated Publishers, 1942), 1: 354.

Parts I and II of this essay were originally written for inclusion in the *Encyclopedia
of Religion in America,* ed. Charles H. Lippy and Peter W. Williams (New York:
Scribner's, 1986).

could not read or write, and the few who could were almost always forced to apply what they believed about God to the survival and liberation of their people rather than to consider it systematically.

No theme has been more prominent in black religious thought than the justice of God. Blacks have always believed in the living presence of the God who establishes the right by punishing the wicked and liberating their victims from oppression. Everyone will be rewarded and punished according to their deeds, and no one—absolutely no one—can escape the judgment of God, who alone is the sovereign of the universe. Evildoers may get by for a time, and good people may suffer unjustly under oppression, but "sooner or later, . . . we reap as we sow."

The "sooner" refers to present, historically observable events: punishment of the oppressors and liberation of the oppressed. The "later" refers to the divine establishment of justice in the "next world," where God "gwineter rain down fire" on the wicked and where the liberated righteous will "walk in Jerusalem just like John." In black religious thought God's justice is identical with the divine liberation of the weak—if not "now" then in the "not yet." Because whites continued to prosper materially as they increased their victimization of blacks, black religious thought came to speak more often of the "later" than of the "sooner."

The themes of justice and liberation are closely related to the idea of hope. The God who establishes the right and puts down the wrong, the God who liberates the oppressed is the sole basis of the hope that the suffering of the oppressed will be eliminated. Black people's hope is based on their faith in God's promise not to "leave the little ones alone in bondage." Indeed, their faith in the coming justice of God is the chief reason blacks have been able to hold themselves together in their struggles for freedom, even though the odds are usually against them.

The ideas of justice, liberation, and hope should be seen in relation to the important theme of love. Theologically God's love is prior to the other themes. But in order to separate black reflections on love from a similar theme in white theology, it is important to emphasize that love in black religious thought is usually linked with God's justice, liberation, and hope. God's love is made known through divine righteousness, liberating the poor for a new future.

God's creation of all persons in the divine image bestows sa-

credness upon human beings and thus makes them the children
of God. To violate any person's dignity is to transgress "God's
great law of love." We must love the neighbor because God has
first loved us. And because slavery and racism are blatant denials
of the dignity of the human person, God's justice means that "he
will call the oppressors to account."

Despite the strength of black faith, belief in God's coming
justice and liberation was not easy for black people. Their suffering created the most serious challenge to their faith. Why did God
permit millions of blacks to be stolen from Africa and enslaved in
a strange land? No black person has been able to escape the
existential agony of that question.

Justice, liberation, hope, love, and suffering represent the major themes in the history of black religious thought. In this essay, I
will examine black religious thought in the light of these themes,
beginning with its origin in slavery and its subsequent development in the activity of black churches and the civil rights movement and in the recent writings on black theology from the 1960s
to the present.

The Origin of Black Religious Thought: Slavery

Black religious thought in North America achieved its distinctive
theological identity in the context of the European enslavement
of African people. Unlike Europeans who came to North America in search of freedom in religion and other aspects of life,
Africans came on slaveships and were forced to carve out some
sense of meaning in the environment of the auction block and the
whip. In a strange land, where they had no rights as human
beings, African slaves had to develop a system of religious beliefs
and practices that would affirm their humanity.

In African traditional beliefs, reality was viewed as a single
system with no sharp distinction between the secular and the
sacred. In some sense everything one did should be in service to
the divine. The worship of African slaves in the Americas consist-
ed in giving appropriate adoration to the High God or Supreme
Being, lesser divinities, and ancestors in the expectation that they
would soon return to their homeland. Many Africans believed
that death would be the gateway to their reincarnation in Africa.
These beliefs and ideas gave structure and meaning to the African world, and they served as the theological starting point for

African captives in the Americas. In Latin America and the Caribbean, African elements were clearly present in the theology and worship of black slaves. To this day one finds the Candomblé in Brazil, Santeria in Cuba, Shango in Trinidad, Obeah in Jamaica, and Voodoo in Haiti. Few scholars deny that the African diaspora in Latin America and the Caribbean carried to the New World African styles of worship, African patterns of religious music and dance, African magical and folk beliefs, and—most importantly for cultural continuity—African religious institutions and sacred offices.

In North America, however, white slaveholders did not permit Africans to practice their religion openly. White slaveholders readily perceived the connection between African religion and slave insurrections. Calculated suppression, along with other unfavorable conditions, greatly reduced the practice and influence of the African tradition. Nevertheless African elements survived in the slaves' music, speech, and thought patterns. Africanisms were also found in the rhythm of dance and the emotional structure of the slaves' existence. When slaves were introduced to Christianity, they reinterpreted what they received in the light of their African past, their present need for dignity and worth, and their future longings for a world in which they would be recognized and treated as human beings.

Black religious thought is neither exclusively Christian (when the latter is defined by the dominant theologies of the West) nor primarily African (when compared with past or contemporary African beliefs). It is both—but reinterpreted for and adapted to the life-situation of black people's struggle for justice in a nation whose social, political, and economic structures are dominated by a white racist ideology.

The tension between "African" and "American" (which has always been associated with the public meaning of "Christian") is deeply embedded in the history of black reflections and practices in religion. In his *Souls of Black Folk,* W. E. B. DuBois's classic statement remains the best description of this paradox: "It is a peculiar sensation, this double-consciousness. . . . One ever feels his two-ness,—an American, a Negro; two souls, two thoughts, two unreconciled strivings; two warring ideals in one dark body, whose dogged strength alone keeps it from being torn asunder."[2]

2. DuBois, *The Souls of Black Folk* (New York: Fawcett, 1968), pp. 16-17.

The "two warring ideals" that DuBois described in 1903 have been at the center of black religious thought from its origin to the present day. It is found in the heated debates about "integration" and "nationalism" and in the attempt to name the community—beginning with the word "African" and using at different times such terms as "Colored," "Negro," "Afro-American," and "Black." Because it is an unresolved tension, it is the source of both the creative contribution that black religion has made toward black liberation and also a serious theological impediment in the struggle for justice. It was the "African" side of black religion that helped slaves to see beyond the white distortions of the gospel and to discover its true meaning as God's liberation of the oppressed from bondage. It was the "Christian" element in black religion that helped slaves to reorient African religion so that it would become useful in their struggle to survive with dignity in the fight against forces of destruction in their community.

Although the African and Christian elements have been found throughout the history of black religious thought, the Christian part gradually became dominant. Though less visible, the African element continued to play an important role in defining the core of black religion, thus preventing it from becoming merely an imitation of Protestant or Catholic theologies in the West.

Of course, there are many similarities between black religious thought and white Protestant and Catholic reflections on the Christian tradition. But the differences between them are perhaps more important than the similarities. The similarities are found at the point of a common Christian identity, and the differences can best be understood in light of the differences between African and European cultures in the New World. While whites used their cultural perspective to dominate others, slaves used theirs to affirm their dignity and to empower themselves to struggle for justice. The major reason for the differences between black and white religion is found at the point of the great differences in life. If religion is inseparably connected with life, then one must assume that slaves' and slaveholders' religious experiences did not have the same meaning because they did not share the same life. They may have used the same words in prayer, song, and testimony or even preached similar sermons. But slaves and slaveholders could not mean the same thing in their verbal and rhythmic expressions because their social and political realities were radically different.

Black slaves nurtured their distinctive religion in intimate communication between friends and within families as well as in larger secret meetings. Scholars refer to this clandestine religious activity as the "invisible institution" or the secret church. The need for secret meetings was created by the restrictions against Africans assembling without the presence of whites and also by black people's dissatisfaction with the worship and preaching in white churches. While the great majority of white Christians condoned slavery, saying it was permitted or even ordained by God, black slaves contended that God willed their freedom and not their servitude. Although they knew they were risking a terrible beating or perhaps even death, slaves nonetheless found it necessary to "steal away" into the woods at night in order to sing, preach, and pray for their liberation from slavery. In these secret meetings was born not only the major slave insurrections but also a black version of the gospel that was consistent with their search for freedom.

Even when slaves worshiped with their masters, it was usually out of a necessity to put on a "good front" so that the master would think of them as pious and religious. The "real meetin'" and the "real preachin'" was held in the swamp, out of the reach of the patrols. An ex-slave, Litt Young, tells of a black preacher who preached "obey your master" as long as her mistress was present. When the mistress was absent, she said, "he came out with straight preachin' from the Bible."[3]

It was in the context of these secret meetings that the slave songs (often called the "Negro Spirituals") were born. The slave songs, like so many black sermons and prayers, stressed the theme of God as the liberator of the oppressed.

> Go down, Moses,
> Way down in Egyptland
> Tell old Pharaoh
> To let my people go.

A similar theme of liberation is found in "Joshua fit de battle of Jericho," "Oh Mary, don't you weep," and "My Lord delivered Daniel."

---

3. See *Life Under the "Peculiar Institution": Selections from the Slave Narrative Collection,* ed. Norman Yetman (New York: Holt, Rinehart & Winston, 1970), p. 337.

The slaves' religious songs also expressed the other themes of black religious thought mentioned earlier, including God's judgment against the oppressors. As one slave expressed it, "White folk's got a heap to answer for the way they've done to colored folks! So much they won't never *pray it* away!"[4] Black slaves also expressed the same point in such songs as "Dere's no hidin' place down here" and "You shall reap jes what you sow." They believed that the wicked will be punished in hell:

> Then they'll cry out for cold water
> While the Christians shout in glory
> Saying Amen to their damnation
> Fare you well, fare you well.

As there was no justice without punishment of the wicked in hell, so there was no liberation of the oppressed without the reward of heaven. Heaven was connected with the theme of hope. Though black slaves longed for God's liberation in this world, their extreme situation of suffering did not make their physical deliverance a realistic expectation in most cases. Accordingly, their hope of liberation was projected into God's eschatological future.

Because many scholars have given a misleading emphasis upon the "otherworldly" quality of black religion, it is important to point out that heaven for many slaves referred not only to a transcendent reality beyond time and space but also designated the earthly places that they regarded as lands of freedom, particularly Africa, Canada, and the northern United States. Frederick Douglass wrote about the double meanings of these songs: "A keen observer might have detected in our repeated singing of 'O Canaan, sweet Canaan, / I am bound for the land of Canaan,' something more than the hope of reaching heaven. We meant to reach the *North,* and the *North* was our Canaan."[5] However, for those slaves who had no chance of escape, heaven referred to that reality that enabled them to affirm their somebodiness even though they were treated like nobodies in this world. Heaven symbolized the slaves' hope in their future liberation, a time when

---

4. See *Dear Ones at Home: Letters from Contraband Camps,* ed. Henry Swint (Nashville: Vanderbilt Press), p. 124.

5. Douglass, *Life and Times of Frederick Douglass* (Secaucus, N.J.: Citadel Press, 1962), p. 159.

their suffering would come to an end. They looked forward to the time when they would "cross the river of Jordan" and "sit down at the welcome table," "talk with the Father," "argue with the Son," and "tell them about the world we just come from."

The dominant emphases of justice, liberation, and hope are closely related to the idea of love. In the religion of the slaves, love can be seen in the absence of bitterness toward whites and in references to their own accounting in the day of judgment. When the slaves talked about the accounting that whites had to give in the day of judgment, it was not because they hated whites but because they believed in the righteousness of God. When they sang "Everybody talking about heaven ain't going there," they were referring not only to whites but also to many slaves whose lives contradicted the commandments of God. According to black slaves, God is no respecter of persons and loves all the same. God's love is best revealed in Jesus, whose meaning is summarized in the gospel of John: "For God so loved the world, that he gave his only begotten Son, that whosoever believeth in him should not perish, but have everlasting life" (3:16, KJV).

Love and suffering belong together in black religious thought. On the one hand, God loves those who suffer; but, on the other hand, if God loves black slaves, why do they suffer so much? This paradox stands at the heart of black faith. Moses and Job, liberation and slavery, cross and resurrection—these polarities are held in dialectical tension, somewhat analogous to DuBois's analysis of the double-consciousness—"an American, a Negro." But unlike the unresolved tension in black people's cultural identity, their faith in the love of God clearly outweighed the doubt created by their suffering. The reason is God's suffering in Jesus.

In the suffering of Jesus, black slaves experienced an existential solidarity with him: "Were you there when they crucified my Lord?" and "he never said a mumblin' word." They also experienced Jesus' solidarity with them. Jesus was present with them as their companion in their misery and their liberator from it into a resurrected existence: "There is a balm in Gilead, to make the wounded whole." While this faith did not cancel out the pain of enslavement, it bestowed upon them a knowledge of themselves that transcended white America's definition of them as slaves. To be sure, they sang "sometimes I feel like a motherless child," and "nobody knows the trouble I've seen," but because they were confident of God's eschatological liberation, they could add (in

the same songs!) "Glory Hallelujah!" The "Glory Hallelujah!"
was not a denial of trouble; it was an affirmation of faith: God is
the companion and liberator of sufferers.

> Weep no more, Martha,
> Weep no more, Mary,
> Jesus rise from de dead,
> Happy Morning.

Black Religious Thought and Black Churches

In addition to creating the invisible institution among slaves in
the South, blacks also founded independent churches, mainly in
the North, beginning in the late eighteenth century. Like the
secret meetings of slaves in the South, the independent black
church movement is additional evidence of the difference between black faith and white religion. When Richard Allen and
Absalom Jones walked out of St. George Methodist Episcopal
Church in Philadelphia in 1787 because they refused to accept
segregation and discrimination, it was the beginning of a separatist church movement among blacks of the North that led to the
founding of the African Methodist Episcopal Church (AME) in
1816, the African Methodist Episcopal Zion Church (AMEZ) in
1821, the Colored Methodist Episcopal Church (CME) in 1870,
and many Baptist churches during the same period.

It is unfortunate that the black separatists did not write creeds
or doctrines to define theologically the difference between black
faith and the white churches from which they separated. The
failure to reflect intellectually on the meaning of their faith has
led many black Christians to assume that there was no theological
difference between white and black views of the gospel, as if what
one does has nothing to do with the definition of faith itself.

While the absence of intellectual reflections on the faith is
unfortunate, it is nevertheless understandable. Since most blacks
in the North, like the slaves in the South, did not have the oppor-
tunity to acquire formal theological training or the time and space
to develop those skills on their own, they did not comprehend
fully the theological consequences of their actions for faith. What
Richard Allen and others perceived and expressed emphatically
with their actions was that segregation in the "Lord's House" was
"very degrading and insulting" and that they were not going to

accept it. Reflecting on the event, Allen said, "We all went out of the church in a body, and they were no more plagued with us in the church."[6]

The idea of blacks separating from whites in order to do things on their own, founding independent institutions, was a revolutionary act in the minds of both blacks and whites of that time. Even many radical white abolitionists and other black supporters rejected such an idea. For blacks to do things on their own meant they could think on their own as well. Blacks began to realize that unless they could demonstrate that they were capable of operating their own churches, it would be even more difficult to make a case for black freedom in the society. White slavemasters realized how revolutionary black separatism was and therefore declared the independent black churches illegal in many parts of the South.

The independent black church movement became one of the major bearers of black religious thought. The themes of justice, liberation, hope, love, and suffering are found in the writings and preaching of persons in the northern black churches. Blacks used their churches not only for preaching and singing about God's justice and liberation but also for coping with the social, political, and economic needs of their community.

Their African heritage and their life-situation in America prevented black ministers from making a sharp separation between the material and spiritual needs of their people. Therefore, it was not by chance that the First National Negro Convention was held at Bethel Church in Philadelphia (1830), where Richard Allen served as the pastor. The African Methodist Episcopal Zion Church was so deeply involved in the abolitionist movement that it became known as the "Freedom Church." Many black churches were used as underground railroad stations for runaway slaves.

Not all blacks in the North separated from white churches. Some remained in order to fight racism in the "Lord's House" as well as in society at large. They included such persons as David Walker, Henry Highland Garnet, Nathaniel Paul, Alexander Crummell, and Francis Grimke.

The writings of black Christians in white churches have left an important body of theological literature that shows clearly the

6. *The Life Experience and Gospel Labors of the Right Rev. Richard Allen* (Nashville: Abingdon Press, 1960), pp. 24-25.

differences between black faith and white religion, even when they remained in the same churches. Differences were found on the issue of slavery and what should be done about it. Henry Highland Garnet, a Presbyterian minister, and David Walker, a Methodist layperson, were the most radical and best known. Walker's "Appeal" (1829) and Garnet's "Address to the Slaves of the United States of America" (1843) shocked even such radical abolitionists as William Lloyd Garrison. Both claimed that Christianity and slavery were radically inconsistent, and that the slaves themselves must strike the blow for freedom because God demanded it. Addressing slaves, Garnet wrote,

> It is as wrong for your lordly oppressors to keep you in slavery, as it was for the man thief to steal our ancestors from the coast of Africa. You should therefore now use the same manner of resistance, as would have been just in our ancestors, when the bloody foot prints of the first remorseless soul thief was placed upon the shores of our fatherland. . . . Liberty is a spirit sent out from God, and like its great Author, is no respecter of persons.[7]

In addition to addressing the slaves concerning their responsibility to resist slavery and telling whites about the terrible consequences in store for them, black preachers also put some questions to God. The central theological question was: Why did the God of liberation, justice, and love permit millions of Africans to be stolen from their African homeland and enslaved in North America? Nathaniel Paul framed the issue in this manner:

> Tell me, ye mighty waters, why did ye sustain the ponderous load of misery? Or speak, ye winds, and say why it was that ye executed your office to waft them onward to the still more dismal state; and ye proud waves, why did you refuse to lend your aid and to have overwhelmed them with your billows? Then should they have slept sweetly in the bosom of the great deep, and so have been hid from sorrow. And, oh'thou immaculate God, be not angry with us, while we come into thy sanctuary, and make the bold inquiry in this thy temple, why it was that thou didst look on with calm indifference of an uncon-

---

7. Garnet, in *Walker's "Appeal" and Garnet's "Address to the Slaves of the United States of America,"* American Negro: His History and Literature Series (New York: Arno Press, 1969), p. 93.

cerned spectator, when thy holy law was violated, thy divine
authority despised and a portion of thine own creatures reduced to a state of mere vassalage and misery?[8]

The question of theodicy was the dominant question not only
during the period of slavery but also throughout the nineteenth
century, because the exploitation of blacks did not end with the
Civil War. Indeed, after the infamous Hayes Compromise of
1877, blacks had less protection from the brutality of whites than
they had during the slavery era. Not only were blacks politically
disenfranchised but the violence of white hate groups was visited
on any black person whom they perceived as asserting equality
with whites. Between 1889 and 1899, 1,240 blacks were lynched.
More than 240 years of slavery, followed by a brutal form of legal
segregation, augmented by the violence of white hate groups,
forced black Christians to probe deeply into why God allowed it to
happen.

Two texts served as the loci for interpreting black history in the
nineteenth century: the book of Exodus and Psalm 68:31. Blacks
identified with the Israel of the Exodus text, and that helped to
blunt the edge of slavery, since they, like Israel, would be liberated. But this answer did not satisfy all, as suggested by J. Sella
Martin in 1865: "Has Providence so little care for human lives as
to permit the sacrifice of over a million of them for the purpose of
overthrowing the system of slavery, only that its victims may be
treated worse than slaves after they are free?"[9] The continuation
of black suffering pushed black religious thought beyond Exodus
to Job and thus into the realm of mystery.

The text to which blacks most often appealed for an explication of their destiny was Psalm 68:31: "Princes shall come out of
Egypt, and Ethiopia shall soon stretch forth her hands unto
God." With this text, they believed they had the answer regarding
the divine purpose of black suffering. Its obscurity enabled blacks
to give a variety of interpretations. Some used it to refute the
charge of black inferiority by identifying "the African race" with
the ancient civilizations of Egypt and Ethiopia as exemplars of a
glorious African past. Others used it to say that God permitted
blacks to be enslaved so they could receive education, elevation,

8. Paul, in *Negro Orators and Their Orations,* ed. Carter G. Woodson (New York:
Russell & Russell, 1925), p. 69.
9. Martin, in the 26 August 1865 issue of the *Christian Recorder.*

and regeneration by Europeans in order that they might not only redeem the African race but Africa itself. As early as 1808, Absalom Jones said, "Perhaps his [God's] design was, that a knowledge of the gospel might be acquired by some of their [slaves'] descendants, in order that they might be qualified to be the messengers of it, to the land of their fathers."[10]

The persistence of black suffering after the Civil War caused the great majority of black ministers to withdraw from political engagement and to devote most of their time to strictly ecclesiastical matters. Many scholars have described this period as the "deradicalization of the black church." The institutionalization of the church, combined with the movement of blacks in great numbers from the rural South to the cities of the North, encouraged many ministers to concentrate on spiritual matters. The churches acquired a conservative posture, becoming closely identified with the accommodation philosophy of Booker T. Washington and concentrating almost exclusively on internal church affairs. The themes of liberation, justice, hope, love, and suffering were interpreted to support their withdrawal from the political struggle for justice. Love became the dominant emphasis with a focus on Jesus in terms of patience, humility, meekness, peacefulness, longsuffering, kindness, and charitableness. They transferred those virtues to blacks, emphasizing their Christ-likeness in contrast to the imperialism, racism, and materialism of whites. Levi Coppin, editor of the AME *Church Review,* said in 1890, "It is my solemn belief, that if ever the world becomes Christianized . . . it will be through the means, under God of the *Blacks,* who are now held in wretchedness, and degradation, by the white *Christians* of the world."[11]

There were several exceptions to this conservative posture of black religious thought, including the positions propounded by Henry M. Turner, the controversial nationalist Bishop of the AME Church; Reverdy C. Ransom, an early advocate of socialism and later elected a bishop in the AME Church; and George Wash-

10. Jones, "A Thanksgiving Sermon Preached January 1, 1808, in St. Thomas's or the African Episcopal, Church, Philadelphia: An Account of the Abolition of the African Slave Trade . . . ," in *Early Negro Writing,* ed. D. Porter (Boston: Beacon Press, n.d.), p. 340.

11. Coppin, cited by A. J. Raboteau in "'Ethiopia Shall Soon Stretch Forth Her Hands': Black Destiny in Nineteenth-Century America," University Lecture in Religion presented at Arizona State University, 27 January 1983, p. 12.

ington Woodbey, a Baptist minister and one of the few blacks who was a dues-paying member of the Socialist Party. Bishop Turner fought fiercely for justice, refusing to accommodate himself to any form of discrimination in the churches or in society. When the Supreme Court ruled in 1883 that the Civil Rights Act of 1875 was unconstitutional, Turner said that the Constitution was a "dirty rag, a cheat, a libel and ought to be spit upon by every Negro in the land."[12] He was a major opponent to the accommodationist philosophy of Booker T. Washington and urged blacks to emigrate to Africa since they could not get justice in the U.S.

But these exceptions were not enough to change the dominant emphasis of black religious thought as defined by the churches. No persons were more cognizant of this than the few ministers who were seeking to address the social and political problems of the black community. "I get mad and sick," writes Bishop Turner, "when I look at the possibilities God has placed within our reach, and to think we are such block-heads we cannot see and utilize them."[13]

12. Turner, in *Respect Black: The Writings and Speeches of Henry McNeal Turner*, ed. Edwin S. Redkey (Salem, N.H.: Ayer, 1971), p. 63.
13. Turner, in *Respect Black*, p. 122.

Black Religious Thought in American History
Part II: More Recent History

The Civil Rights Movement and Martin Luther King, Jr.

THE WITHDRAWAL OF THE BLACK CHURCH FROM POLITICS CREATED the conditions that gave rise to the civil rights movement: the National Association for the Advancement of Colored People (NAACP) in 1909, the National Urban League (NUL) in 1911, and the Congress for Racial Equality (CORE) in 1942. These national organizations, and similar local and regional groups in many parts of the United States, took up the cause of justice and equality of blacks in the society. They were strongly influenced by ideas and persons in the churches. Civil rights organizations not only internalized the ideas about justice, liberation, hope, love, and suffering that had been preached in the churches; they also used church property to convene their own meetings and usually made appeals for support at church conferences. The close relations between the NAACP and black churches has led some to say that "the black church is the NAACP on its knees."

Due to the deradicalization of the black church, progressive black ministers found it difficult to remain involved in the internal affairs of their denominations. Baptist ministers, because of the autonomy of their local congregations, found it easier than the Methodists did to remain pastors while also being deeply involved in the struggle for black equality in the society. Prominent examples included Adam Clayton Powell and Adam Clayton Powell, Jr., father and son pastors of Abyssinian Baptist Church in New York. Adam Jr. made his entry onto the public stage by leading a four-year nonviolent direct-action campaign, securing some ten thousand jobs for Harlem blacks. In 1944 he was elected to Congress.

Adam Clayton Powell, Jr., embraced that part of the black religious tradition that refused to separate the Christian gospel from the struggle for justice in society. In his influential book *Marching Blacks,* he accused the white churches of turning Christianity into "churchianity," thereby distorting the essential message of the gospel which is "equality" and "brotherhood."

> The great loving heart of God has been embalmed and laid coolly away in the tombs we call churches. Christ of the Manger, the carpenter's bench, and the borrowed tomb has once again been crucified in stained-glass windows.[1]

Other influential thinkers of this period included Howard Thurman and Benjamin E. Mays. Howard Thurman wrote twenty-two books and lectured at more than five hundred institutions. He also served as dean of Rankin Chapel and professor of theology at Howard University, as the dean of Marsh Chapel and minister-at-large of Boston University, and as minister and co-founder of the interdenominational Fellowship Church of San Francisco. His writings and preaching influenced many, and *Life* magazine cited him as one of the twelve "Great Preachers" of this century. Some of his most influential writings include *Deep River* (1945), *The Negro Spiritual Speaks of Life and Death* (1947), *Jesus and the Disinherited* (1949), and *The Search for Common Ground* (1971). Unlike most black ministers concerned about racial justice, liberation, love, suffering, and hope, Thurman did not become a political activist; he took the "inward journey" (the title of one of his books), focusing on a "spiritual quest" for liberation beyond race and ethnic origin. He was able to develop this universalist perspective without ignoring the urgency of the political issues involved in the black struggle for justice.

Benjamin E. Mays, ecumenist and long-time president of Morehouse College, also made an important contribution to black religious thought through his writings and addresses on the black church and racism in America. He was the author (with Joseph W. Nicholson) of *The Negro's Church* (1933), *The Negro's God* (1938), *Seeking to be Christian in Race Relations* (1957), and *Born to Rebel* (1971). He also chaired the National Conference on Religion and Race in 1963. Mays was an example of a black religious thinker who found the black church too limiting as a context for

---

1. Powell, *Marching Blacks,* rev. ed. (New York: Dial Press, 1973), p. 194.

confronting the great problems of justice, liberation, love, hope, and suffering. Like Thurman and Powell, Mays regarded racism as anti-Christian, an evil that must be eliminated from the churches and the society.

No thinker has made a greater impact upon black religious thought or even upon American society and religion as a whole than Martin Luther King, Jr. The fact that many white theologians can write about American religion and theology with no reference to him reveals both the persistence of racism in the academy and the tendency to limit theology narrowly to the academic discourse of seminary and university professors.

Much has been written about the influence of King's graduate education upon his thinking and practice, especially the writings of George Davis, Henry David Thoreau, Mahatma Gandhi, Edgar S. Brightman, Harold DeWolf, G. W. Hegel, Walter Rauschenbusch, Paul Tillich, and Reinhold Niebuhr. Of course, these religious and philosophical thinkers influenced him greatly, but it is a mistake to assume that they constituted the basis of his life and thought. King was a product of the black church tradition; its faith determined the essence of his theology. He used the intellectual tools of highly recognized thinkers to explain what he believed to the white public and also to affirm the universal character of the gospel. But he did not arrive at his convictions about God by reading white theologians. On the contrary, he derived his religious beliefs from his acceptance of black faith and his application of it to the civil rights struggle.

In moments of crisis, King turned to the God of black faith. From the beginning of his role as the leader of the Montgomery bus boycott to his tragic death in Memphis, King was a public embodiment of the central ideas of black religious thought. The heart of his beliefs revolved around the ideas of love, justice, liberation, hope, and redemptive suffering. The meaning of each is mutually dependent on the others. Though love may be appropriately placed at the center of his thought, he interpreted it in the light of justice for the poor, liberation for all, and the certain hope that God has not left this world in the hands of evil men.

King often used the writings of Tillich, Niebuhr, and other white thinkers to express his own ideas about the interrelations of love and justice. But it was his internalization of their meaning in the black church tradition that helped him to see that "unmerited suffering is redemptive." While those who fight for justice must be prepared to suffer in the struggle for liberation, they must never inflict suffering on others. That was why King described nonviolence as "the Christian way in race relations" and "the only road to freedom."

To understand King's thinking, it is necessary to understand him in the context of his own religious heritage. His description of himself is revealing:

> I am many things to many people; Civil Rights leader, agitator, trouble-maker and orator, but in the quietness of my heart, I am fundamentally a clergyman, a Baptist preacher. This is my being and my heritage for I am also the son of a Baptist preacher, the grandson of a Baptist preacher and the great-grandson of a Baptist preacher. The Church is my life and I have given my life to the Church.[2]

The decisive impact of the black church heritage upon King can be seen in his ideas about justice, liberation, love, hope, and suffering. He took the democratic tradition of freedom and combined it with the biblical tradition of justice and liberation as found in the book of Exodus and the prophets. Then he integrated both traditions with the New Testament idea of love and suffering as disclosed in Jesus' cross, and from all three, he developed a theology that was effective in challenging all Americans to create the beloved community in which all persons are equal. While it was the Gandhian method of nonviolence that provided the strategy for achieving justice, it was, as King said, "through the Negro church" that "the way of nonviolence became an integral part of our struggle."[3]

As a Christian whose faith was derived from the cross of Jesus, King believed that there could be no true liberation without suffering. Through nonviolent suffering, he contended, blacks would not only liberate themselves from the necessity of bitterness and feeling of inferiority toward whites but would also prick the conscience of whites and liberate them from a feeling of superiority. The mutual liberation of blacks and whites lays the foundation for both to work together toward the creation of an entirely new world.

---

2. King, "The Un-Christian Christian," *Ebony*, August 1965, p. 77.
3. King, "Letter from Birmingham Jail," in *Why We Can't Wait* (New York: Signet, 1963), p. 87.

In accordance with this theological vision, King initially rejected Black Power because of its connotations of hate; he believed that no beloved community of blacks and whites could be created out of bitterness. He said that he would continue to preach nonviolence even if he became its only advocate.

He took a similar but even more radical position with regard to the war in Vietnam. Because the Civil Rights Act (1964) and the Voting Rights Bill (1965) did not significantly affect the life-chances of the poor, and because of the dismal failure of President Johnson's War on Poverty, King became convinced that his dream of 1963 had been turned into a nightmare. Gradually he began to see the connections between the failure of the war on poverty and the expenditures for the war of Vietnam. In the tradition of the Old Testament prophets and against the advice of many of his closest associates in black and white communities, King stood before a capacity crowd at Riverside Church and condemned America as "the greatest purveyor of violence in the world today."[4] He proclaimed God's judgment against America and insisted that God would break the backbone of U.S. power if the nation did not bring justice to the poor and peace to the world. Vicious criticisms came from blacks and whites in government, civil rights groups, and the nation generally as he proclaimed God's righteous indignation against the three great evils of our time—war, racism, and poverty.

During the severe crises of 1966-68, King turned not to the theologians and philosophers of his graduate education but to his own religious heritage. It was eschatological hope derived from his slave grandparents and mediated through the black church that sustained him in the midst of grief and disappointment. This hope also empowered him to "master [his] fears" of death and to "stand by the best in an evil time." In a sermon he preached at Ebenezer Baptist Church, he said,

> I've decided what I'm going to do; I ain't going to kill nobody
> . . . in Mississippi . . . and . . . in Viet Nam, and I ain't going to
> study war no more. And you know what? I don't care who
> doesn't like what I say about it. I don't care who criticizes me in
> an editorial; I don't care what white person or Negro criticizes
> me. I'm going to stick with the best. . . . Every now and then we

---

4. King, *The Trumpet of Conscience* (New York: Harper & Row, 1968), p. 24.

sing about it, if you are right, God will fight your battle. I'm
going to stick by the best during these evil times.[5]

It was not easy for King to "stand by the best," because he often
stood alone. But he firmly believed that the God of black faith had
said to him, "Martin Luther, stand up for righteousness. Stand
up for justice. Stand up for truth. And lo, I will be with you, even
until the end of the world."[6]

King combined the exodus-liberation and cross-love themes
with the message of hope found in the resurrection of Jesus. He
derived hope not from the optimism of liberal Protestant theology but from his belief in the righteousness of God as defined
by his reading of the Bible through the eyes of his slave forerun-
ners. The result was the most powerful expression in black history of the essential themes of black religious thought from the
integrationist viewpoint.

> Centuries ago Jeremiah raised a question, "Is there no balm in
> Gilead? Is there no physician?" He raised it because he saw the
> good people suffering so often and the evil people prospering.
> Centuries later our slave foreparents came along and they too
> saw the injustices of life and had nothing to look forward to
> morning after morning, but the rawhide whip of the overseer,
> long rows of cotton and the sizzling heat, but they did an amaz-
> ing thing. They looked back across the centuries and they took
> Jeremiah's question mark and straightened it into an exclama-
> tion point. And they could sing, "There is a balm in Gilead to
> make the wounded whole. There is a balm in Gilead to heal the
> sinsick soul."[7]

Black Power and Black Theology

From the time of its origin in slavery to the present, black
religious thought has been faced with the question of whether to
advocate integration into American society or separation from it.
The majority of the participants in the black churches and the
civil rights movement have promoted integration, and they have

5. King, "Standing by the Best in an Evil Time," unpublished sermon no. 7,
King Center Archives.
6. King, "Thou Fool," unpublished sermon no. 14, King Center Archives.
7. King, "Thou Fool."

interpreted justice, liberation, love, suffering, and hope in the light of the goal of creating a society in which blacks and whites can live together in a "beloved community."

While integrationists have emphasized the American side of the double consciousness of African-Americans, there have also been nationalists who rejected any association with the United States and instead have turned toward Africa. Nationalists contend that blacks will never be accepted as equals in a white racist church and society. Black freedom can be achieved only by black people separating themselves from whites—either by returning to Africa or by forcing the government to set aside a separate state within the United States so blacks can build their own society.

The nationalist perspective on the black struggle for freedom is deeply embedded in the history of black religious thought. Its prominent advocates include Bishop Henry McNeal Turner of the AME Church; Marcus Garvey, the founder of the Universal Negro Improvement Association; and Malcolm X of the religion of Islam. Black nationalism is centered on blackness, a repudiation of all of the values of white culture and religion. Proponents reverse the values of the dominant society by attributing to black history and culture what whites have said about theirs. For example, Bishop Turner claimed that "We have as much right biblically and otherwise to believe that God is a Negro . . . as you . . . white people have to believe that God is a fine looking, symmetrical and ornamented white man."[8] Marcus Garvey held a similar view: "If the white man has the idea of a white God, let him worship his God as he desires. . . . We Negroes believe in the God of Ethiopia, the everlasting God—God the Father, God the Son and God the Holy Ghost, the One God of all ages."[9]

The most persuasive interpreter of black nationalism during the 1960s was Malcolm X, who proclaimed a challenging critique of King's philosophy of integration, nonviolence, and love. Malcolm X advocated black unity instead of the "beloved community," self-defense in lieu of nonviolence, and self-love in place of turning the other cheek to whites.

Like Turner and Garvey, Malcolm X asserted that God is

8. Turner, in *Respect Black: The Writings and Speeches of Henry McNeal Turner*, ed. Edwin S. Redkey (Salem, N.H.: Ayer, 1971), p. 176.

9. Garvey, in *Philosophy and Opinions of Marcus Garvey*, ed. Amy Jacques-Garvey, Studies in American Negro Life Series (New York: Atheneum, 1969), p. 44.

black; but unlike them he rejected Christianity as the white man's religion. He became a convert initially to Elijah Muhammad's Nation of Islam and later to the world-wide Islamic community. His analysis of Christianity and of American society as white was so persuasive that many blacks followed him into the religion of Islam, and others accepted his criticisms even though they did not become Muslims. Malcolm pushed civil rights activists to the left and caused many black Christians to reevaluate their interpretation of Christianity.

> Brothers and sisters, the white man has brainwashed us black people to fasten our gaze upon a blond-haired, blue-eyed Jesus! We're worshiping a Jesus that doesn't even *look* like us! Now, just think of this. The blond-haired, blue-eyed white man has taught you and me to worship a *white* Jesus, and to shout and sing and pray to this God that's *his* God, the white man's God. The white man has taught us to shout and sing and pray until we *die*, to wait until *death*, for some dreamy heaven-in-the-hereafter, when we're *dead*, while this white man has his milk and honey in the streets paved with golden dollars right here on *this* earth![10]

During the first half of the 1960s, King's interpretation of justice as equality with whites, liberation as integration, and love as nonviolence dominated the thinking of the black religious community. However after the riot in Watts in August 1965, black clergy began to take another look at Malcolm's philosophy, especially his criticisms of Christianity and American society. Malcolm X's contention that America was a nightmare and not a dream began to ring true to many black clergy as they watched their communities go up in flames as young blacks shouted in jubilation, "burn, baby, burn."

It was during the James Meredith "march against fear" in Mississippi in June 1966 (after Malcolm had been assassinated in February 1965) that some black clergy began to openly question King's philosophy of love, integration, and nonviolence. When Stokely Carmichael proclaimed "Black Power," it sounded like the voice of Malcolm X. Though committed to the Christian gos-

---

10. Malcolm X, *Autobiography of Malcolm X* (New York: Ballantine Books, 1973), p. 222.

pel, black clergy found themselves moving slowly from integration to separation, from Martin Luther King to Malcolm X.

The rise of Black Power created a decisive turning point in black religious thought. Black Power forced black clergy to raise the theological question about the relation between black faith and white religion. Although blacks have always recognized the ethical heresy of white Christians, they have not always extended it to Euro-American theology. With its accent on the cultural heritage of Africa and political liberation "by any means necessary," Black Power shook black clergy out of their theological complacency.

Unable to ignore or reject Black Power, a small group of black clergy, mostly from the North, separated themselves from King's absolute commitment to nonviolence. Neverthless, like King and unlike Black Power advocates, these black clergy were determined to remain within the Christian community. They were faced with the dilemma of how to reconcile Christianity and Black Power, Martin Luther King and Malcolm X.

In their attempt to resolve their dilemma, an ad hoc National Committee of Negro Churchmen (later the National Conference of Black Churchmen—NCBC) published a statement on "Black Power" in the *New York Times*, 31 July 1966. The publication of the "Black Power" statement represented the beginning of a process in which a radical group of black clergy in both black and white denominations made a sharp separation between their understanding of the Christian gospel and the theology of white churches. Addressing the leaders of white America (especially the churches) and the black community, black clergy endorsed the positive elements in Black Power.

In the debate that followed, the clergy of the NCBC became certain that their theological orientation in black history and culture created in them a view of the gospel radically different from that of white Christians. The term "liberation" emerged as the dominant theme in black theology, and justice, love, hope, and suffering were interpreted in the light of its political implications. Black clergy were determined that they would not allow the theology of white racists to separate them from their solidarity with suffering blacks in the urban ghettos. That was why they found Malcolm X more useful than King, even though they were as determined as King not to separate themselves from the latter.

Writings in the general area of black theology began with the public statements of the NCBC, in which blacks attacked racism in the white church as heresy. Also important for the development of black theology was the contribution of Vincent Harding. In his essays "Black Power and the American Christ" (1967) and "The Religion of Black Power" (1968), Harding articulated the religious meaning of Black Power and the challenge it posed for the followers of Martin Luther King.

In 1968, Albert Cleage published a book of sermons with the provocative title *The Black Messiah*. The contents were as controversial as the title. Unlike Bishop Henry Turner and Marcus Garvey, Cleage advocated that Jesus and God were literally black. His theological position became known as "Black Christian Nationalism." He attempted (unsuccessfully) to convince Black Power advocates that they were the church (even though they were not religiously conscious of it), and he tried to make the clergy of NCBC understand that the only true church was the black liberation struggle. Cleage interpreted the ideas of liberation, justice, and love exclusively in terms of the philosophy of black separatism.

Although NCBC and Albert Cleage endorsed Black Power, it was not until 1969 that I wrote the first book on black theology, a work entitled *Black Theology and Black Power*. Less radical than Cleage but somewhat to the left of NCBC, I agreed with both in identifying the gospel of Jesus with God's liberation of the poor and the weak. I defined white theology as heretical and referred to Black Power's message of liberation as the true gospel for twentieth-century America.

In my second book, *A Black Theology of Liberation* (1970), I made the word *liberation* the organizing principle of an emerging black perspective on theology. On the one hand, I was unlike Cleage in that I remained in dialogue with other perspectives on the Christian faith; on the other hand, I was like Cleage in that I interpreted the themes of justice, love, suffering, and hope according to the political liberation of the black poor.

Other black theologians and clergy of NCBC supported me in my definition of Christian theology as a theology of liberation. Shortly after the publication of *Black Theology and Black Power*, the Theological Commission of NCBC assembled a group of black clergy and theologians in Atlanta (June 1969) to write a statement on "Black Theology." They defined it as "a theology of black liberation," and they also connected it with James Forman's "Black Manifesto" (which had been issued a month earlier at Riverside Church in New York) by endorsing the concept of reparations.

In 1972, two important texts on black theology appeared: J. Deotis Roberts's *Liberation and Reconciliation: A Black Theology* and Major Jones's *Black Awareness: A Theology of Hope.* Both Roberts and Jones supported the concept of black theology as liberation theology, but they felt that my emphasis on liberation was too narrow and my attack on white people was too severe. Roberts balanced the idea of liberation with reconciliation, and Jones balanced my "by any means necessary" with an ethic of nonviolence. Both attempted to develop a black theology that was not dependent on Black Power and thus did not exclude whites from the Christian community in the struggle to build a just society. Roberts and Jones appealed to the life and writings of Martin Luther King for their claims about the gospel and the black struggle of freedom, while I turned to Malcolm X.

No issue affected the development of black theology more than the question of its relation to African history and culture. This issue was introduced in theology in a provocative manner with the publication of Joseph R. Washington's *Black Religion* (1964). He claimed that black religion was a unique, non-Christian folk religion derived from the African heritage and the black struggle for social and political betterment. He also deplored the black separation from Christianity and blamed it on white Christians. While most black theologians spoke against Washington's book, especially his low evaluation of black religion, several agreed with him about the importance of the African heritage in black religious development. Charles Long, Gayraud Wilmore, Cecil Cone, and others went on to offer a related criticism of black liberation theology. Because I and other radical black theologians accented liberation and did not mention the importance of the African heritage of black theology, the critics contended that the liberation theologians needed to recognize and correct their dependence upon the supposedly heretical European theologians. If black theology is to be truly black, it must derive its meaning from the history and culture of the people in whose name it claims to speak. This critique was substantially incorporated into black liberation theology, particularly in my books *The Spirituals and the Blues* (1972), *God of the Oppressed* (1975), and subsequent writings. I began to turn away from my former use of white theologians to a greater use of slave narratives, sermons, prayers, and songs as the chief sources for the development of the themes of justice, liberation, love, suffering, and hope in black theology.

The most challenging critique of black liberation theologians came from the writings of William R. Jones, who asked the provocative question, "Is God a white racist?" In a book with that question as its title, Jones asked, If God is liberating the black oppressed from bondage, what is the evidence for that claim? Although Jones's analysis posed a serious challenge for all religions of salvation, the way he put the question gave it a special poignancy for blacks. Black theologians could not ignore or belittle it.

Of course there was no answer to Jones's question that would meet the demands of his philosophical structure. But his critique forced black theologians to face head-on the problem of suffering. His questioning made them realize that suffering must be the controlling category of black theology along with liberation, so that black professors could not easily identify liberation with any particular realization in history. Black theologians responded to Jones by focusing more intentionally on the theme of hope as King had earlier. Using Scripture and the black experience, they contended that in the cross of Jesus, God takes the suffering of the victims upon himself, and in the resurrection of Jesus, evil is overcome. The victims can now know that their humanity is not negated by their victimization.

Although black theologians debated among themselves about liberation and reconciliation, African religion and Christianity, liberation and suffering, they agreed that white religion is racist and therefore un-Christian. In black theologians' attack on white religion and in their definition of the gospel as liberation, they moved toward a close solidarity with liberation theologians in Africa, Asia, Latin America, and the oppressed in the United States. In the early seventies, the dialogues between black and Third World theologians began—first with Africans, then with Latin Americans, and lastly with Asians. The dialogues with Third World theologians on other continents created a realization of the need for dialogue between blacks and other oppressed minorities in the United States and with an emerging feminist consciousness in all Christian groups.

The dialogues with other liberation theologians has revealed both the strengths and weaknesses of black theology. For example, Africans pointed out the gaps in the knowledge of American black theologians about African culture; Latin theologians revealed their lack of class analysis; Asian theologians showed the importance of a knowledge of religions other than Christianity; feminist theologians revealed the sexist orientation of black theology; and other minorities in the United States showed the necessity of a coalition in the struggle for justice in the United States and around the globe.

A black feminist theology has already begun to emerge with the work of such persons as Paula Murray, Jackie Grant, Katie Cannon, Delores Williams, and Kelly Brown. It is clear that black theology will develop radically new directions when a fully developed feminist consciousness emerges. It will deepen its analysis of racism and also protect it from the worse aspects of sexism.

The impact of Third World theologians has already pushed black theology in the direction of a consideration of Marxism and socialism. This exploration has taken place in the context of the Ecumenical Association of Third World Theologians (EATWOT), which held its organizing meeting in Dar es Salaam, Tanzania, in 1976. Since that time meetings have been held in Ghana (1977), Sri Lanka (1979), Brazil (1980), India (1981), and Geneva (1983). Black theologians have also had a positive impact on Third World theologians in accenting the importance of the problem of racism. These dialogues have also established the category of liberation as the heart of the gospel for many Third World theologians here and abroad.

Impact on American Religion

The impact of black religious thought on American religion has been significant. During the slavery era, it challenged the white interpretation of Christianity by creating the "invisible institution" and separatist churches which emphasized God's justice and love as being identical with the liberation of slaves from bondage. When physical liberation seemed impossible, blacks affirmed their humanity by projecting their liberation into God's eschatological future, a time when all wrongs will be righted and evil will be completely exterminated.

From the time of its origin in slavery to its contemporary embodiment in the civil rights and black nationalists movements,

black religious thought has challenged segregation and discrimination in the society and the churches. It has contended that
God's justice and love cannot be reconciled with racism. Black
Christians not only preached and sang about liberation in the
next world but also used their churches as instruments for the
establishment of justice in this one. They also created organizations that supported their churches and sometimes went beyond
them in the fight for the equality of blacks in the society.

Through the life and thought of Martin Luther King, Jr., and
Malcolm X, black religious thought achieved national and international recognition. King is the only American besides George
Washington whose birthday is a national holiday, and he was the
second black American to receive the Nobel Peace Prize. Both
King and Malcolm X laid the foundation that gave birth to black
liberation theology which has become widely known and taught
in many parts of the world.

The significance of black theology for black religious thought
is found at two points. First, black theology identified racism in
the white churches as a Christian heresy, in contrast to the previous tendency to limit its critique to the ethical behavior of white
Christians. Black theology claimed that the faith of white Christians was defective because of their indifference to and support of
racism in their churches and the larger society.

Second, by rejecting white theology as heresy, the proponents
of black theology were also forced to create a new theology of the
black poor, one that would empower them in their struggle for
justice. Black theologians began to reread the Bible in the historical context of the black experience of struggle. From this new
hermeneutical vantage point emerged the theological conviction
that the God of Moses and the prophets and of Jesus and Paul is
none other than the liberator of the poor and the downtrodden.
With its articulation of this theological insight, black theology
became known not only as the first expression of liberation theology in North America, but more importantly it located the chief
meaning of liberation in the cross of Jesus, so as to say with Paul
that "God chose what is foolish in the world to shame the wise,
God chose what is weak in the world to shame the strong, God
chose what is low and despised in the world, even things that are
not, to bring to nothing the things that are" (1 Cor. 1:27-28).

What Is the Church?

MUCH HAS BEEN WRITTEN ABOUT THE CHURCHES DURING THE course of their historical development. Ernst Troeltsch, H. Richard Niebuhr, and Peter Paris have written about the social origin and teaching of the Christian churches.[1] Others, such as Williston Walker, Carter G. Woodson, E. Franklin Frazier, and Sydney Ahlstrom, have concentrated on their institutional history.[2] Systematic and historical theologians such as Karl Barth, Cyril Richardson, Jürgen Moltmann, and Hans Küng have focused their attention on the doctrine of the church, with special interest in its transcendent origin.[3] None of these foci should be isolated from the others, because each is important for the formulation of a meaningful, contemporary definition of the church.

Every generation of Christians should ask: What is it that constitutes our identity and thus empowers us to live it out in the world? To answer this question, we must focus on the institutional and ethical activity that validates our ecclesiological confessions. If we separate the doctrine of the church from its historical embodiment in our congregational life, we will also ignore the

---

1. See Troeltsch, *The Social Teaching of the Christian Churches,* 2 vols., trans. Olive Wyon (New York: Harper & Row, 1960); Niebuhr, *The Social Sources of Denominationalism* (Cleveland: Meridian Books, 1957); and Paris, *The Social Teaching of the Black Churches* (Philadelphia: Fortress Press, 1985).

2. See Walker, *A History of the Christian Church,* rev. ed. (New York: Scribner's, 1959); Woodson, *History of the Negro Church* (Washington: Associated Publishers, 1921); Frazier, *The Negro Church in America* (New York: Schocken Books, 1964); and Alstrom, *A Religious History of American People* (New Haven: Yale University Press, 1972).

3. See Barth, *Church Dogmatics,* ed. Geoffrey W. Bromiley and T. F. Torrance, trans. Geoffrey W. Bromiley, (Edinburgh: T. & T. Clark, 1956), 4/1-2; Richardson, *The Church through the Centuries* (New York: Scribner's, 1950); Moltmann, *The Church in the Power of the Spirit* (New York: Harper & Row, 1977); and Küng, *The Church* (New York: Sheed & Ward, 1967).

This essay was presented at a Pastors' Conference on the Church at Emory University (1968) and later rewritten for a conference on Jesus and Justice at Philander Smith College (1985).

social and political significance of our credal formulations. Therefore, whatever else we may advance as our definition of the church, we should never separate the doctrine of the church from specific local congregations. A theological doctrine of the church attempts to point to "more" than what can be empirically observed in local congregations, but this theological "more" is itself obscured and distorted when it is separated from particular congregations and their behavior in the world. This means that the "more" which may be disclosed in a theology of the church can only be found through a critical social analysis of the churches.

What then is the relationship between *the* church and local congregations, between a theology of the church and a sociology of the churches? Unfortunately theologians have tended to give an inordinate amount of attention to the doctrine of the church, an ecclesiological perspective that seems to exist nowhere in society except in their minds and textbooks. This clever ecclesiological sophistry enables pastors and other church officials to justify existing church institutions without seriously inquiring about their historical faithfulness to the gospel message that they claim as the foundation of the church's identity. By focusing their attention on a doctrinal understanding of the church that has little sociological relevance, theologians can ignore obvious historical contradictions and shortcomings of empirical churches. This abstract theological maneuver makes it possible for theologians to speak of the church as the "body of Christ" without saying a word about its relation to broken human bodies in society.

Focusing on the sociology of the churches, including their privileged political status in this society, makes it possible for church people to see themselves as others see them and thus partly guard against fatuous theological speech. Too often churches have been guilty of covering up their own sins behind sophisticated theological jargon. While saying that we are concerned about the poor, we do not analyze and fight against the socio-economic structures responsible for their poverty. To be sure, many congregations have food programs, jail and hospital ministries, and other special projects designed to "help" the needy and the unfortunate ones. But such projects are not designed to challenge the capitalist system that creates human misery. Churches are often incapable of attacking the root cause of oppression because they are beneficiaries of the socio-political system responsible for it. It is because churches are so much a reflection of the values of the society in which they exist that they also have a serious credibility problem among people who regard their poverty and imprisonment as a by-product of an unjust social order. A poem entitled "Listen Christians" that was circulated at a poor people's rally in Albuquerque, New Mexico, describes a perspective of the church that church people do not like to hear.

> I was hungry
> and you formed a humanities club
> and you discussed my hunger.
> Thank you.
>
> I was imprisoned
> and you crept off quietly
> to your chapel in the cellar
> and prayed for my release.
>
> I was naked
> and in your mind
> you debated the morality of my appearance.
>
> I was sick
> and you knelt and thanked God for your health.
>
> I was homeless
> and you preached to me
> of the spiritual shelter of the love of God.
>
> I was lonely
> and you left me alone
> to pray for me.
> You seem so holy;
> so close to God.
> But I'm still very hungry
> and lonely
> and cold.
>
> So where have your prayers gone?
> What have they done?
> What does it profit a man
> to page through his book of prayers
> when the rest of the world
> is crying for his help?

This poem exposes the hypocrisy of the churches and forces one to ask whether any ecclesial confession is ever valid apart from a concrete, practical activity that validates it. How can one speak about the church as the body of the crucified Jesus of Nazareth when church people are so healthy and well-fed and have no broken bones? Can we really claim that established churches are the people of God when their actions in society blatantly contradict the one who makes that identity possible?

In this essay, it is not my intention to ridicule the churches. I am a member of the church, and I have been one of its ministers since I was sixteen years old, with pastorates in Little Rock at San Hill, Spring Hill, and Allen Chapel African Methodist Episcopal Churches. It is because of my love and concern for the church that I, as one of its theologians, must subject it to severe criticism when it fails to be in society what it confesses in worship. Our so-called theological jargon about the church has become so insensitive to human pain and suffering that it distorts the theologian's authentic Christian calling. In this situation it would be helpful to return to the concrete social reality of our existence, so that we may be permitted to move to a deeper theological level. I do not believe that we can experience the deeper level of our theological identity until we have immersed ourselves in the social matrix in which our identity must be actualized. For this reason, a social analysis of the churches must precede a doctrine of the church. We should never allow a theological interpretation of the church's transcendent origin to obscure the empirical behavior of churches that deny what church people affirm in their ecclesiological confessions.

While a sociology of the churches should serve as the starting point for an analysis of the theology of the church, it nonetheless is important to point out that theology and sociology in the context of the church and the churches are not identical. Despite what some persons might think, I still believe in the transcendent foundation of the church. I only wish to emphasize that I think that we church people, especially theologians and pastors, have been too carried away by that theological option and as a result have distorted its true meaning. The transcendent origin of the church has been used as a camouflage to cover up the gross shortcomings of so-called Christian churches. Are church people not claiming much too much when they say that what they represent is of God when their actions clearly originate from the values of a racist, classist, and sexist society?

Furthermore, even if it is agreed that the church has its origin beyond the context of this world, it is still necessary to face honestly the issue of the relation between the theology of the church and a sociology of the churches. The way out of this dilemma is not a bold theological affirmation that "the Christian church is the Church of Jesus Christ." Rather, the acid test of any ecclesiological statement is whether it has taken sufficient account of the actual world in which liturgical confessions are made. For the transcendent can be encountered only in the particularity of a human situation. Whatever else the transcendent may mean, it is always relevant to and for human beings. This is the significance of the Incarnation, God becoming human in Jesus. It is the Incarnation that necessitates our sociological starting point. To be sure, the sociological without the theological reduces the church to a social club of like-minded people. But the theological without a critical sociological component makes the church a non-historical, spiritual community whose existence has no effect on our social and political environment. In this essay, my concern is to examine the theological understanding of the church in the context of its socio-political existence in the world.

The Interrelationship of the Church, Jesus Christ, and the Poor

The Christian church is that community of people called into being by the life, death, and resurrection of Jesus. The beginning and the end of the church's identity is found in Jesus Christ and nowhere else. He is the subject of the church's preaching, and he embodies in his person the meaning of its mission in the world. To ask "What is the church?" is also to ask "Who is Jesus?" for without Jesus the church has no identity. That was why Paul referred to the church as the body of Christ and also why many theologians, past and present, would adhere to the claim that every ecclesiological statement is at the same time a christological statement.

The differences among the churches, therefore, have not arisen from the issue of whether Christ is to be regarded as the head of the church: all churches that bear the name "Christian" adhere to the confession that "Jesus Christ is Lord." Rather, the differences among the churches that prevent their unity arise from their understanding of the theological and sociological implications of that christological confession. When the churches begin to spell out the structural meanings of Jesus' Lordship for congregational life and for participation in society, they often find themselves in sharp disagreement. What does it mean to declare that Jesus is the head of the church whose sovereignty extends to the whole world? Not all churches answer that question in the same way.

Another factor worth noting has been the churches' inordinate preoccupation with the *theological* side of their identity, as if their transcendent origin legitimated their privilege in society and also bestowed upon their ministry a similar privilege in judgment regarding how the society should be politically, socially, and economically arranged. From the early church to the present, there have been intense debates regarding the precise meaning of the *ekklesia*. But the discussions have focused primarily on the church's specifically *divine* origin in order to defend its privilege against "heretics" rather than in defense of the poor which the divine origin entails. This distorted emphasis on the theological, almost to the exclusion of the need to make political solidarity with the poor and against their oppressors, has often blinded churches to their responsibility to implement in society what they sometimes confess in worship.

In his debate with the Donatists, Augustine, for example, defined the church in terms of the four marks of unity, holiness, catholicity, and apostolicity, with an emphasis also on its visible and invisible nature. John Calvin and his supporters of the magisterial Reformation added the two additional marks of "the Word of God purely preached and heard and the sacraments administered according to Christ's institution."[4] The Radical Reformation added several additional marks, one of which was obedience to the "Cross of Christ which is borne for the sake of his testimony and Word."[5] Menno Simons, a representative of this Radical tradition, rejected the inordinate emphasis on the invisibility of the church. He maintained that "as long as the transgressors and willful despisers of the holy Word are unknown to

---

4. Calvin, *Institutes of the Christian Religion*, 4.1.9.

5. Simons, *The Complete Writings of Menno Simons*, trans. Leonard Verduin (Scottdale, Pa.: Herald Press, 1956), p. 741.

the church she is innocent, but when they are known and then not excluded after proper admonition, but allowed to remain in the fellowship . . . then . . . she ceases to be the church of Christ."[6] It was a concern of Simons and other Anabaptists to *restore* the church along the lines of its apostolic pattern. That was why *discipline* became one of the essential marks of the church. Unlike Augustine and Calvin, who contended that the true church was invisible and thus known only to God by virtue of divine election, the Anabaptists insisted that the church of Christ is an "assembly of the pious." While Calvin could say that "the pure ministry of the Word and pure mode of celebrating the sacraments" are sufficient for the church's identity "even if it otherwise swarms with many faults,"[7] Simons contended that "we know for sure where . . . there is no pious Christian life, no brotherly love, and no orthodox confession, there no Christian church is."[8]

While there are sharp differences between Augustine and Calvin on the one hand and Menno Simons and his Anabaptist supporters on the other, there is a striking similarity among them from the perspective of their concentrated preoccupation with the theological or the transcendental origin of the church. This transcendent focus has often prevented church people from seeing the correct relationship between theology and politics, the preaching of the gospel to the poor and its implementation in society. During the sixteenth century, the Anabaptists appeared to come the closest to recognizing the cross of Jesus as essential for the church's life of suffering. They insisted that "the True Church was a suffering church whose changing patterns were ever cast in the shadow of the Man Upon the Cross."[9] But unfortunately they tended to become too sectarian by withdrawing from social and political responsibility and thereby reinforcing the idea that the church is a specifically spiritual institution.

It was Karl Marx and later the sociologists of knowledge who pointed out that the churches' emphasis on the specifically theological was in fact a camouflage for their support of the existing social order. The churches are not really nonpolitical, even though they often have said that "the church should stay out of

6. Simons, *The Complete Writings of Menno Simons*, p. 746.
7. Calvin, *Institutes*, 4.1.12.
8. Simons, *The Complete Writings of Menno Simons*, p. 752.
9. Franklin H. Littell, *The Origins of Sectarian Protestantism* (New York: Macmillan, 1964), p. 53.

politics." As the active participation of the Moral Majority in elec-
toral politics has demonstrated, this dictum holds true for many
white conservative church people only as long as the existing
social order is not disturbed. If a threat to the "law and order" of
the system exists, the churches will take the lead in providing a
sacred justification for all so-called good people to take up arms
against the forces of evil.

It was because the churches and their leaders provided a theological justification for an unjust social order that Marx defined
religion as the opiate of the people. Whether Marx was correct in
his judgment is still a much-debated issue, with church people
insisting that they represent more than a "sacred canopy" of their
social environment.[10] Regardless of what church people claim
about themselves in their worship and intellectual life, it seems
that the burden of proof is upon them to validate their claims of
transcendence. And this validation must involve more than intellectual or pious appeals to God. Church people must be able to
point to something in their congregational life that is not simply a
religious legitimation of the values of the social order in which
they live.

The need for the church to act against itself in order to be its
true self has been pointed out by both theologians and social
ethicists. For example, Langdon Gilkey has said that "since the
church is *in* secular culture, . . . the life of the congregation cannot in any sense express transcendence of the culture around it
unless it is willing to challenge the injustice . . . of the wider community in which it lives."[11] With a firmer grasp of the tools of
social analysis, James Gustafson is even more insightful in his
comments about the churches. Gustafson is concerned about the
sharp distinction made between the public and private life and
the limitation of the church to the latter. But even in the private
sphere, he says, the church's "role has become supportive,
therapeutic, pastoral and even idolatrous, for it functions to give
religious sanctions to a culturally defined pattern of life that is
itself not sufficiently subjected to theological and moral criticism."[12] One test of the authenticity of the church's claim to

10. On this, see Peter Berger, *The Sacred Canopy* (Garden City, N.Y.: Double-
day-Anchor, 1969).

11. Gilkey, *How the Church Can Minister to the World without Losing Itself* (New
York: Harper & Row, 1964), p. 71.

12. Gustafson, *The Church as Moral Decision-Maker* (Philadelphia: Pilgrim Press,
1970), p. 63.

transcendence is its capacity to represent in its congregation a "socially heterogeneous" people. If it is not possible for blacks and whites to worship and practice the Christian faith in the world as *one* community because of radically different cultural mores, can we not conclude that their respective racial groupings are due to each people's values and not due to the work of God's Spirit? Jesus Christ breaks down the barriers that separate people (Gal. 3:21).

> The physical presence of heterogeneity makes it more difficult for a congregation to confuse a particular social mode of life with the religiously acceptable and divinely ordained one. . . . Moral concerns brought under the conditions of social and cultural diversity could not be simply the projection of the ideology of a particular interest group on the screen of divine approval.[13]

It is unfortunate that Gilkey's and Gustafson's points about transcendence have not been forcefully advanced so as to shake up the social and political complacency of white churches. Established white churches have almost always focused on the specifically theological understanding of their identity, which also has usually led to a conservative approach to politics, especially in race relations. One can examine the attitude of white churches toward African slavery and find that with few exceptions their views functioned as a religious legitimation of their social and political interests. Many whites openly justified slavery as ordained of God, quoting Paul's admonition "slaves be obedient to your master" as the evidence. Others, being a little more sophisticated, ignored the issue altogether, as if one's attitude toward human servitude had nothing to do with the gospel of Jesus. Another group, while admitting that slavery was immoral and should be abolished, advocated a gradual, peaceful approach to its abolition. It is revealing that similar attitudes were found among white church people regarding lynching, school integration, civil rights, Black Power, and poverty. With regard to justice and peace for persons who are not of European descent, the great majority of white church people (conservative and liberal, right and left, theologians, pastors, and laypeople) seem to reflect in their religion the values of the existing racist and capitalist socioeconomic order.

13. Gustafson, *The Church as Moral Decision-Maker*, pp. 122, 123.

Gustafson explains the support of white clergy and theologians of the existing social order in this way:

> Like all beings, the clergy and the theologians are more comfortable if they can blame what is wrong on forces outside themselves. . . . Clergy and theologians can find as good excuses as any man to deny any responsibility for what is happening to the community and mission with whose leadership they are charged. If there is any sense of repentance, it is all too often, like a general confession of sin, vague and undifferentiated. It leads to a certainty of guilt for the ills of the Church but does not move in the direction of overcoming those ills.[14]

I believe that whatever the Christian faith may be, it is never a reflection of the values of the dominant culture. That was why God elected Hebrew slaves and not Egyptian slavemasters as the covenant people. That was also why the prophets defined God's justice as punishment of the oppressor and the liberation of the poor. In a similar vein but at a much deeper level, the birth, life, teachings, death, and resurrection of Jesus mean that God turns the world's value system upside down. No one expressed this point any clearer than the apostle Paul:

> It was to shame the wise that God chose what is foolish by human reckoning, and to shame what is strong that he chose what is weak by human reckoning; those whom the world thinks common and contemptible are the ones that God has chosen—those who are nothing at all to show up those who are everything.
>
>   1 Corinthians 1:27-28, JB

If the white churches expect to be taken seriously about their claim to be of God, then they must begin to act against the social order and ecclesiastical structures that do not affirm the humanity of people of color.

It is important to note the contrast between black and white churches in the United States during the slavery era and the time of the civil rights movement in the 1950s and '60s. For example, when white preachers and missionaries introduced their version of Christianity to African slaves, many slaves rejected it, contending that God willed their freedom and not their servitude. Sepa-

---

14. Gustafson, *The Church as Moral Decision-Maker*, p. 151.

rate and independent black congregations began to develop among slaves and free Africans in the North and South, because black people did not believe that a segregated congregational life in which they were treated as second-class Christians was reconcilable with their view of the Lordship of Jesus over the church. If Jesus Christ is the Lord of the church and the world as white confessions claimed, then church institutions that claim the Christian identity must reflect their commitment to him in the congregational life of the church as well as in its political and social involvement in society. When northern black Methodists and Baptists formed independent church institutions in Philadelphia, New York, and Baltimore, and when southern blacks created a secret, "invisible institution" in Alabama, Georgia, Arkansas, and Mississippi, their actions in both contexts suggested that some black people recognized the connection between theology and politics, between the confession of faith in church worship and the political commitment that validated it in society. Expressing her reaction to the sermons of white preachers, Hanna Austin, an ex-slave from Georgia, said, "We seldom heard a true religious sermon: but we were constantly preached the doctrine of obedience to masters and mistresses."[15] One white preahcer interpreted Christian obedience to black slaves in this way: "The Lord says . . . if you are good to your masters and mistresses, He has got a kitchen in heaven and you will all go there by and by."[16]

But African slaves knew that God had more than a kitchen waiting for them, and their experience of this "eschatological more" in Jesus Christ necessitated the formation of a congregational life so that their christological encounter could be liturgically celebrated. Minnie Ann Smith, an ex-slave, reflected on her presence in the church as an "invisible," secret, but historical institution: "We slips off and have prayer but daren't 'low the white folks to know it and sometimes we hums 'ligious songs low like when we's working. It was our way of prayin' to be free, but the white folks didn't know it."[17] In this quotation, a different perspective on the invisible church is suggested. It is an invisibility

15. Austin, cited by Olli Alho in *The Religion of the Slaves: A Study of the Religious Tradition and Behavior of Plantation Slaves in the United States, 1830-1865* (Helsinki: Soumalainen Tiedeakatemia, 1976), p. 140.
16. *The Religion of the Slaves*, p. 170.
17. Smith, cited in *The Religion of the Slaves*, p. 125.

grounded not (as with Augustine and Calvin) in divine election but in a religious conviction about the Lordship of Christ that had to be lived out in history and in the midst of an extreme situation of political oppression.

It is unfortunate that many contemporary black churches have strayed from their liberating heritage. Instead of deepening their commitment to the poor in their community and in the Third World, many have adopted the same attitude toward the poor as have the white churches from which they separated. Too many black churches are more concerned about buying and building new church structures than they are about feeding, clothing, and housing the poor. Too many pastors are more concerned about how to manipulate people for an increase in salary than they are about liberating the oppressed from socio-political bondage. If black churches do not repent by reclaiming their liberating heritage for the empowerment of the poor today, their Christian identity will be no more authentic than that of the white churches that segregated them.

It is revealing that the modern search for unity among the churches is focused on *confessional* unity and that neither white nor black churches of United States object to that limited focus. When the World Council of Churches (WCC) was organized in Amsterdam in 1948, its unity was based on the confession of "Jesus Christ as God and Savior." There was no reference to the political and social significance of this confession. But the subsequent increase of Asians, Africans, and Latin Americans as member churches has called this narrow theological understanding of the church into question. It is not that Third World Christians reject the christological focus of the WCC. On the contrary, they insist that the christological confession must be validated by a political commitment that is necessitated by it. In the christologies of Asian, African, and Latin American liberation theologies,[18]

18. Although liberation theology is largely associated with the church in Latin America, it is important to emphasize that similar developments are found in the churches and theologies of Africa, Asia, and among minorities and women in the United States. The best sources for an examination of these theologies and their relationship to each other are the books that have been produced by the Ecumenical Association of Third World Theologians (EATWOT). EATWOT was organized in 1976 in Tanzania and has held subsequent meetings in other countries of the Third World, focusing on African, Asian, and Latin American liberation theologies. See *The Emergent Gospel*, ed. Sergio Torres and Virginia Fabella

Jesus Christ is not defined principally with the sort of substance language of Greek philosophy found in the Nicean and Chalcedonian definitions of 325 and 451. For many Third World theologians, Jesus is the Liberator,[19] who came, as the gospel of Luke says,

> to bring good news to the poor,
> to proclaim liberty to the captives
> and to the blind new sight,
> to set the downtrodden free,
> to proclaim the Lord's year of favour.
>
> 4:18, JB

The church is that people who have been called into being by the life, death, and resurrection of Jesus so that they can bear witness to Jesus' Lordship by participating with him in the struggle of freedom. This means that the primary definition of the church is not its confessional affirmations but rather its political commitment on behalf of the poor.

To liberate the poor requires social analysis that explains the origin and nature of human poverty. Why are people poor, and who benefits from their poverty? This question places the church in the context of society and forces it to be self-critical as it seeks to realize its mission of bearing witness to God's kingdom that is coming in and through the human struggles to liberate the poor. The church bears witness to Christ's Lordship not only in preaching about justice but also in being the agent for its implementation in society.

(Maryknoll, N.Y.: Orbis Books, 1978); *African Theology en Route*, ed. Kofi Appiah-Kubi and Sergio Torres (Maryknoll, N.Y.: Orbis Books, 1979); *Asia's Struggle for Full Humanity*, ed. Virginia Fabella (Maryknoll, N.Y., Orbis Books, 1980); *The Challenge of Basic Christian Communities*, ed. Sergio Torres and John Eagleson (Maryknoll, N.Y., Orbis Books, 1981); and *Irruption of the Third World*, ed. Virginia Fabella and Sergio Torres (Maryknoll, N.Y.: Orbis Books, 1983). Orbis Books is well known for its publications of books on liberation theologies in the Third World and also among minorities in the United States.

19. See Leonardo Boff, *Jesus Christ Liberator: A Critical Christology for Our Time*, trans. Patrick Hughes (Maryknoll, N.Y.: Orbis Books, 1978); Hugo Echegaray, *The Practice of Jesus*, trans. M. J. O'Connell (Maryknoll, N.Y.: Orbis Books, 1980); my *God of the Oppressed* (New York: Seabury Press, 1975); and Bishop Joseph A. Johnson, Jr., "Jesus Christ: Liberator," in his *The Soul of the Black Preacher* (Philadelphia: United Church Press, 1970).

The Church as the Servant of God's Coming Future

If Jesus Christ is Lord of the church, then the church is his servant. It is that congregation of people whose identity as the people of God arises from a definition of servanthood that is derived from Jesus' life, death, and resurrection. By definition, the church exists for others, because its being is determined by the One who died on the cross for others.

The others for whom the church exists are the poor and not the rich, the downtrodden and oppressed and not the proud and the mighty. Because the church is a community called into being by the "Crucified God,"[20] it must be a crucified church, living under the cross.

The servanthood of the church is defined by the cross of Jesus, and nothing else. To be a servant of the crucified One is to be his representative in society, bearing witness (in words, actions, and suffering body) to the kingdom that Jesus revealed in his life, death, and resurrection. We must be careful not to spiritualize servanthood so as to camouflage its concrete, political embodiment. Being a servant of Jesus involves more than meeting together every Sunday for worship and other liturgical gatherings. It involves more than serving as an officer or even a pastor of a church. Servanthood includes a political component that thrusts a local congregation in society, where it must take sides with the poor. Servanthood is a call to action that commits one to struggle for the poor.

Servanthood is the opposite of the world's definition of lordship. That was why Jesus said to his disciples,

> You know that among the pagans their so-called rulers lord it over them, and their great men make their authority felt. This is not to happen among you. No; anyone who wants to become great among you must be your servant, and anyone who wants to be first among you must be slave to all.
>
> Mark 10:42-44, JB

The task of the church is more than preaching sermons about justice and praying for the liberation of all. The church must be the agent of justice and liberation about which it proclaims. A confessional affirmation of peace is not enough. The church must represent in its congregational life and seek to structure in

20. See Jürgen Moltmann, *The Crucified God* (New York: Harper & Row, 1974).

society the peace about which it speaks. When a congregation does not even attempt to structure in its life and in the society the gospel it preaches, why should anyone believe what it says? "To affirm that [people] are persons and as persons should be free, and yet do nothing tangible to make this affirmation a reality, is a farce."[21]

It is the cross of Jesus that connects the church with the victim. "We cannot speak of the death of Jesus until we speak of the real death of people," writes Gustavo Gutiérrez. Unnecessary starvation in Ethiopia, staggering poverty throughout the world, and rich American churches continue to sing and pray to Jesus as if the gospel has nothing to do with feeding the hungry and clothing the naked. In 1980, the World Bank reported that, "excluding China, approximately 750 million persons live in 'absolute poverty'" of which "40,000 small children die" each day "from malnutrition and infection."[22] All of this is unnecessary. But we live in a nation that is more concerned about using food as "a tool in the kit of American diplomacy," to quote the former U.S. Secretary of Agriculture Earl Butz, than using it to save the lives of starving human beings. The United States feeds people missiles. According to Arthur Simon, the author of *Bread for the World,*

> In 1984 the United States devoured approximately $663 million each day in direct military spending—more than the entire annual budgets of the World Health Organization and the UN Development Program combined. The United States allocates about 40 times more for military defense than it does for development assistance.[23]

With so many people dying in the world, how can the churches continue their organizational routine and still expect sensitive people to believe that they are concerned about the cross of Jesus? That is why Hugo Assmann has said that "the church cannot be the reason for its own existence."[24] To preserve itself is to destroy

21. Paulo Freire, *Pedagogy of the Oppressed* (New York: Herder & Herder, 1970), p. 35.
22. As noted by Arthur Simon in *Bread for the World,* rev. ed. (New York: Paulist Press; Grand Rapids: Eerdmans, 1984), p. 7.
23. Simon, *Bread for the World,* p. 144.
24. Assmann, *Theology for a Nomad Church,* trans. Paul Burns (Maryknoll, N.Y.: Orbis Books, 1975), p. 81.

itself. Nothing is more applicable to the church's identity than
Jesus' claim that the one who would save his or her life shall lose it,
and the one who loses his or her life for my sake shall find it. The
church's distinctive identity is found not in itself but in the crucified Jesus, whose Spirit calls the church into being for service on
behalf of victimized people.

When the church makes its political commitment on behalf of
the poor, the historical actions of the church bear witness to an
ultimate hope grounded in the resurrection of Jesus. The church
is a hoping community. It believes that the things that are can and
ought to be otherwise. How is it possible to hope in hopeless
situations? That is the question that all oppressed people must
face when their projects of freedom end in failure. How can they
believe that they are what they shall be when their history seems
to be closed to the future?

It is in the historical context of an apparent closed future that
Jesus Christ "makes a way out of no way" by creating a people
who believe that because of his resurrection "that which is cannot
be true." This is God's distinctive gift for the oppressed who
otherwise would not have the courage to "keep on keeping on"
even though the odds are against them. Max Weber has expressed this experience of the poor in sociological terms.

> The sense of honor of disprivileged classes rests on some con-
> cealed promise for the future which implies the assignment of
> some function, mission, or vocation to them. What they cannot
> claim to *be*, they replace by the worth of that which they one day
> will *become*. . . . Their hunger for a worthiness that has not fall-
> en their lot . . . produces this conception from which is derived
> the rationalistic idea of a providence, a significance in the eyes
> of some divine authority possessing a scale of values different
> from the one operating in the world of man.[25]

According to Weber, "since every need for salvation is an expression of some distress, social or economic oppression is an
effective source of salvation beliefs."[26] Because the hope for salvation is always related or derived from situations of distress,

25. Weber, *The Sociology of Religion*, trans. Ephraim Fischoff (Boston: Beacon
Press, 1964), p. 106.
26. Weber, *The Sociology of Religion*, p. 107.

Weber has a different sociological evaluation of the religion of privileged classes.

> Other things being equal, classes with high social and economic privilege will scarcely be prone to evolve the idea of salvation. Rather, they assign to religion the primary function of legitimizing their own life pattern or situation in the world. This universal phenomenon is rooted in a certain basic psychological pattern. When a man who is happy compares his position with that of one who is unhappy, he is not content with the fact of his happiness, but desires something more, namely the right to this happiness, the consciousness that he has earned his good fortune, in contrast to the unfortunate one who must equally have earned his misfortune. Our everyday experience proves that there exists just such a psychological need for reassurance as to the legitimacy or deservedness of one's happiness, whether this involves political success, superior economic status, . . . or anything else. What the privileged classes require of religion, if anything at all, is this psychological reassurance of legitimacy.[27]

"Correspondingly different," according to Weber, "is the situation of the disprivileged. Their particular need is release from suffering."[28] They look forward to the time when the things that are no longer will be. Because there is so little in their history that reflects their humanity, they are forced by the unrealized vision in their historical struggle to look beyond history in the hope that the truth which is not present in their situation will soon take place in God's eschatological future.

This eschatological hope of the oppressed is not an opiate or a sedative, because it is a hope derived from historical struggle and never separated from it. God is the power who transforms the suffering of the present into hope for the future. The reality of God's presence in the lives of the poor empowers them to affirm their humanity, by looking to another world where they will be treated as human beings. No people have expressed this eschatological hope with greater depth of apocalyptic imagination than black slaves in North America. The knowledge that who they were was not defined ultimately by their servitude enabled

27. Weber, *The Sociology of Religion*, p. 107.
28. Weber, *The Sociology of Religion*, p. 108.

them to hold themselves together and to fight back. They knew that one day the fighting would be over and they would "walk in Jerusalem just like John." They would "cross the river of Jordan," "sit down at the welcome table." Their knowledge of a new future created by Jesus' resurrection sustained them in their struggle, enabling them to say "nobody knows who I am till the judgment morning."

Black Worship: A Historical-Theological Interpretation

BLACK WORSHIP IS CONNECTED WITH BLACK LIFE, AND IT IS CHARAC-
terized by a religious sense inseparable from the suffering that
determined it. Whether Catholic or Protestant—Methodist, Baptist, or Pentecostal—black worship is not derived primarily from
these theological and historical traditions. To be sure, there are
elements of Catholic and Protestant doctrine and rituals (mostly
Protestant) in black worship. In black congregations of the Methodist and Presbyterian churches, one is likely to find an order of
worship that reflects the content and style of those traditions. But
to use John Wesley's theology or the Westminster Confession as
the hermeneutical key to explain why a black congregation has
adopted the Methodist or Presbyterian denominational structure
is to misunderstand black worship and thus to distort its theological meaning. When black people gather together for worship and praise to God, it is not because they have made a decision
about the theological merits of Luther's Ninety-five Theses or of
Calvin's *Institutes of the Christian Religion*. These are not our ecclesiastical and theological traditions. At most, they are secondary
structures in which God has placed us so that we might "work out
our salvation in fear and trembling."

Since we did not create the various Catholic and Protestant
structures, we cannot use these labels as the primary definition of
our religious experience. Indeed, these white religious structures
are the reason for the black necessity to create a style of worship
that does not deny our essential humanity. A black congregation
may be Methodist, Baptist, or even Catholic, but always with a
difference. And this difference is far more important in the as-
sessment of the meaning of black worship than are the white

This essay originally was presented at a workshop on black worship sponsored by
Black Methodists for Church Renewal (Detroit, 1976).

traditions from which the black church often derives its name.

Black worship has been wrought out of the experience of slavery and lynching, ghettos and police brutality. We have "been 'buked and scorned" and "talked about sho's you borned." In worship, we try to say something about ourselves other than what has been said about us in the white church and the society it justifies. Through sermon, prayer, and song, we transcend societal humiliation and degradation and explore heavenly mysteries about starry crowns and gospel shoes. Our church is the only place we can go with tears in our eyes without anyone asking "what are you crying about?" We can preach, shout, and sing the songs of Zion according to the rhythm of the pain and joy of life, without being subjected to the dehumanizing observations of white intellectuals—sociologists, psychologists, and theologians. In worship we can be who we are as defined by our struggle to be something other than what the society says we are. Accordingly, our gathering for worship is dictated by a *historical* and *theological* necessity that is related to the dialectic of oppression and liberation. Apart from the historical reality of oppression and our attempt to liberate ourselves from it, we would have no reason to sing "My soul looks back and wonders how I got over." To understand the interplay of the past, present, and future as these are expressed in black worship, it is necessary to examine first the historical context that created its unique style and then the theological content that defined its meaning.

The Historical Context of Black Worship

Black worship was born in slavery. What else could the word "black" mean in relation to worship except a description of the historical origin of those assembled. Most black worshipers do not know the details of our historical beginnings. What they know and feel is that they are *black* and therefore connected with Africa, slavery, and the struggle of freedom. Black worship was born on the slaveships and nurtured in the cotton fields of Alabama, Arkansas, and Mississippi. What we believe and how we express it in worship cannot be separated from our African heritage on the one hand and American slavery and Christianity on the other. African life and culture was the bedrock of the African personality. It was that element in the black slaves' being that structured their response to American slavery and the Christian gospel. Black worship was born in the meeting of the West African High God with the God of Moses and Jesus. Black worship was created and formed in the context of American slavery as African slaves sought to create meaning in a completely alien and oppressive environment. In order to keep a measure of sanity in a completely alien and oppressive environment, African slaves had to fashion a theological system of beliefs and create a worship style that did not destroy them physically and mentally.

Initially black worship was determined largely by our African heritage, with an emphasis on the rhythm of our dance and music. There was no separation of the secular and sacred. Reality was viewed as a single system. In some sense, everything one did should be service to the divine, whether directed to the High God, to lesser divinities, or to ancestors. These beliefs and ideas gave structure and meaning to the African world and served as the theological starting point for African captives in the Americas.

In Latin America and the Caribbean, African theology and rituals remained visibly present in black religious structures, including worship. In North America, however, white slaveholders did not permit Africans to practice their religion openly. The intensity and success with which whites destroyed African life and culture has led many scholars to conclude that Africanisms were completely eliminated in the life of the American slaves. It was the studies of Melville Herkovits that changed the course of scholarly debate on this issue. With the publication of his *Myth of the Negro Past,* it was no longer possible to take for granted that everything black slaves did was derived from their oppressors. Although Herkovits was seriously challenged by E. Franklin Frazier and others, it is safe to say that he showed that Africans in North America did preserve some African cultural forms. Beliefs and customs were transmitted by slaves to their descendants, and they are found in our music, speech, and thought patterns. Africanisms are also found in the rhythm of our dance and the emotional structure of our being. When Christianity was introduced to slaves, Africans converted it to their religious heritage, refusing to accept any version of the gospel that did not harmonize with the African spirit of freedom.

This conversion of Christianity by Africans to their life-situation accounts for the fact that white slaveholders had radically different views of the gospel than those held by African slaves. Initially, white masters did not permit their slaves to be Christianized. Some understood that Christian baptism implied manumission, and there were too many biblical references to freedom. But white missionaries and preachers convinced many slave masters that Christianity made blacks better slaves—that is, obedient and docile. As one slaveholder put it, "The deeper the piety of the slave, the more valuable he is in every respect." However, it is important to point out that before the First and Second Great Awakening and the emergence of the Methodists and Baptists, most African slaves remained outside the belief systems of Christianity. Later, when Africans did "convert" to it, their conversion was not identical with the religious conversion of the whites who held them as slaves. That was why the independent black churches were founded in the North and the so-called invisible institution flourished in the South.

The affirmation of some people that there is no difference between black worship and white worship is clearly problematic in light of both historical and contemporary evidence. If worship is inseparably connected with life, then we must assume that the worship services of slaves could not have had the same meaning as the worship services of slaveholders, because they did not share the same life. They may have used the same words in prayer, songs, and testimony, or even preached similar sermons. But slaves and slaveholders could not mean the same thing in their verbal and rhythmic expressions, because their social and political realities were radically different. That was why black slaves organized the first Baptist church in Silver Bluff, South Carolina, between 1773 and 1775 and also why Richard Allen and Absalom Jones walked out of St. George Methodist Church of Philadelphia in 1787. Similar events took place in New York, Baltimore, and other places among black Methodists and Baptists. This same black version of the gospel produced such prophetic persons as Henry Highland Garnet, David Walker, and Nathaniel Paul—all of whom recognized the radical incompatibility of Christianity and slavery. No one expressed this point any clearer than Walker, in his "Appeal" of 1829:

> I ask every [person] who has a heart and is blessed with the privilege of believing—Is not God a God of justice to all his creatures? . . . Then if he gives peace and tranquility to tyrants, and permits them to keep our fathers, our mothers, ourselves and our children in eternal ignorance and wretchedness to

support them and their families, would he be to us a God of justice?[1]

However, even before Walker wrote his famous "Appeal," and prior to the rise of the independent black Baptist and Methodist churches, there was already present an "invisible institution" in the South that emphasized the "overturned pot," the "prayin' ground," and the "hush harbor." An ex-slave preacher described those secret meetings in this manner:

> Meetings back there meant more than they do now. Then everybody's heart was in tune and when they called on God they made heaven ring. It was more than just Sunday meeting and then no more Godliness for a week. They would steal off to the fields and in the thickets and there, with heads together around a kettle to deaden the sound, they called on God out of heavy hearts.[2]

The slaves were searching for a private place where they could sing and shout and there would be nobody there to turn them out. In these secret meetings were born not only the major slave insurrections but also a black version of Christianity that was consistent with their search for freedom.

African slaves refused to accept Christianity as a given datum or as a deposit of fixed doctrines from white missionaries and preachers. Christianity as a rigidly defined system of beliefs about God, Jesus, and the Holy Spirit was inconsistent with the African personality, in which rhythm, passion, and feeling defined the structure of one's being in the world. Therefore, when white Baptists and Methodists arrived on the North American scene in a significant manner during the late eighteenth and early nineteenth centuries, Africans, for the first time during their presence, responded with enthusiasm. This response, contrary to popular opinion, was not to the system of beliefs in either denomination or to a religious consciousness traceable merely to white evangelical Protestantism. African slaves' response to Baptists and Methodists was complex and cannot be reduced to a

1. Walker, in *Walker's "Appeal" and Garnet's "Address to the Slaves of the United States of America,"* American Negro: His History and Literature Series (New York: Arno Press, 1969), p. 16

2. Cited by George P. Rawick in *From Sundown to Sunup* (Westport, Conn.: Greenwood Publishing, 1972), p. 40.

single factor. The appeal of the Methodists and Baptists was partly due to their early antislavery reputation, the opportunities for
black leadership provided by camp meetings, a tolerance for
somatic and ecstatic worship, and an encouragement of the conversion experience. Among the Methodists and Baptists, blacks
were permitted some freedom in worship, reminiscent of their
African heritage and related to their fight against slavery.

Black worship is not white worship, no matter how close the
similarities might be in appearance. Black people have always
known that. It does not matter that white people sometimes copy
our preaching style. Whites may pray, sing, or clap their hands
with a rhythm that makes it difficult for even blacks to make the
distinction. Conversely, no one can deny that white evangelical
Protestantism of the Second Great Awakening, particularly the
revival hymns, did influence the content and style of black worship. One need only point to the popularity of the hymns of Isaac
Watts among black congregations in order to demonstrate that
point. Nevertheless there is a radical difference between black
and white worship services. Both whites and blacks know this, and
that is why even today one seldom finds them worshiping
together.

The source of the difference between black and white worship
services is found at the point of a difference in life. Even when
slaves worshiped with their masters, it was usually out of necessity
to put on a "good front" so that the masters would think of them
as pious and religious. The "real meetin'" and the "real preachin'" was held in the swamp, out of the reach of the patrols. An ex-
slave, Litt Young, tells of a black preacher who preached
"obey your master" as long as her mistress was present. When the
mistress was absent, she said "he came out with straight preachin'
from the Bible."[3]

The need for secret meetings were created by the legal restrictions against African slaves assembling without the presence
of whites and also black people's dissatisfaction with the worship
and preaching of white churches. Although slaves knew they
were risking a terrible beating or perhaps even death, they nonetheless found it necessary to "steal away" into the woods at night
in order to sing, preach, and pray for their liberation from slav-

3. Young, cited by Norman R. Yetman in *Life Under the "Peculiar Institution":
Selections From the Slave Narrative Collection* (New York: Holt, Rinehart & Winston,
1970), p. 337.

ery. Adeline Cunningham, an ex-slave from Texas, reported,

> No suh, we never goes to church. Times we sneaks in de woods
> and prays de Lawd to make us free and times one of de slaves
> got happy and made a noise dat dey heard at de big house and
> den de overseer come and whip us 'cause we prayed de Lawd to
> set us free.[4]

Black slaves had to create their own style of worship. They
shouted and prayed for the time they would "most be done toilin'
here."

Because black people were victims, they could not accept white
people's interpretation of the gospel. The apostle Paul's "slave be
obedient to your master" was a favorite text of white missionaries
and preachers. Hannah Scott of Arkansas expressed her reaction
to one such preacher in this way: "But all he say is 'bedience to the
white folks, and we hears 'nough of dat without him tellin' us."[5]

In order to hear another word and to sing another song, they
held secret worship services in the slave cabin or in the woods at
night. As one ex-slave put it, "Dey law us out of church, but dey
couldn't law 'way Christ."[6] These worship services included singing, preaching, shouting, and conversion. Black slaves used the
"overturned pot" in order to keep from being heard by their
masters or the patrollers. Carey Davenport, a former slave, re-
membered those meetings: "Sometimes the cullud folks go down
in dugouts and hollows and hold they own service and they used
to sing songs what come a-gushing up from the heart."[7] In this
worship context was born their encounter with God, the One they
believed would bring them through. The preacher often spoke
about "dark clouds hanging over their heads" and of the "rocky
roads they have to travel." At other times, he told them about
"deep valleys" and "high mountains," but he assured them that
they had a future not made with human hands. The element of
faith in the righteousness of God prevented black slaves from
accepting despair as the logical consequence of their servitude.

Immediately following the legal abolition of slavery, the "invisible institution" became visible as newly freed blacks joined inde-

4. Cunningham, cited by Rawick in *From Sundown to Sunup*, p. 35.
5. Scott, cited by Eugene Genovese in *Roll Jordan Roll* (New York: Pantheon
Books, 1972), p. 207.
6. Cited by Genovese in *Roll Jordan Roll*, p. 213.
7. Davenport, cited by Rawick in *From Sundown to Sunup*, p. 34.

pendent black churches. What was once done in secret could now be done in the open. Like the secret meetings during the slavery era, black worship after the Civil War was defined by the sermon, song, shout, and the experience of conversion. Each of these elements in black worship was defined by the freedom of the Spirit who moved into the lives of the people, giving them hope and the courage to defend their dignity in an extreme situation of oppression.

An important moment in the history of black worship came during World War I, when many blacks migrated to the cities in search of a measure of freedom in employment and other aspects of black life. Needless to say, most did not find what they had hoped for, and once again they found it necessary to "take their burdens to the Lord and to leave them there." This they did by creating storefront churches and other praise houses of the Lord. This was also the period of the rise of black sects and cults with such figures as Father Divine and Daddy Grace. But more important for black Christian churches was the rise of gospel music with Thomas Dorsey and Mahalia Jackson as dominant personalities. This music put life into the churches by emphasizing the presence of the Spirit.

It was the presence of God's Spirit as defined by gospel music which empowered civil rights activists to fight for justice even though the odds were against them. Because they believed that God was in the black struggle for freedom, they refused to allow George Wallace and Mississippi Klansmen to destroy their faith that "we shall overcome." In Alabama, Mississippi, and Georgia, facing constant terror and death, poor blacks and their supporters kept on marching, singing "woke up this morning with my mind stayed on freedom" and "I ain't gonna let nobody turn me around."

Black worship today is very similar to what it was in the past. The names of the denominations may be new, but the style and content of our worship is very much like that of our grandparents. Instead of singing and preaching in those small southern church houses, we are now proclaiming God's word in storefront churches in New York, Detroit, Philadelphia, and Chicago. We sometimes call the places the "United House of Prayer for All People" or the "Church of What's Happening Now."

From the time of slavery to the present, the black church has been that place where African-Americans could go in order to get some release from the harsh, oppressive realities of the white world. Black people go to church in order to be renewed by God's liberating Spirit. In prayer, sermon, and song, they tell God about "rollin' through an unfriendly world" as a "pilgrim of sorrow" and "motherless child."

> Sometimes I'm up, sometimes I'm down,
> Oh, yes, Lord!
> Sometimes I'm almost to the ground,
> Oh, yes, Lord!

Living in a "troublesome world," "tossed and driven," blacks have been enabled by the felt presence of the Spirit to acknowledge their suffering without being determined by it.

> Oh, nobody knows the trouble I've seen,
> Nobody knows my sorrow.
> Nobody knows the trouble I've seen,
> Glory, Hallelujah!

During the late 1960s, some expressions of black worship began to take on a more "secular" form with no obvious reference to the God of Christian theism. Theater and poetry workshops began to replace the church. An example is the National Black Theatre in Harlem founded by Barbara Ann Teer. Others like Haki R. Madhubuti, Nikki Giovanni, and Gwendolyn Brooks articulated a black spiritual and political message that affirmed the dignity and worth of blacks in their struggle for justice. Some black churches had become too middle-class to accommodate the spirit and aspiration of the Black Power movement. A new form of black ritual was developed wherein the poet became the preacher with a message for the people.

It was in the context of the civil rights and Black Power movements that black theology was born. Black theology is an attempt to show liberation as the central message of the Christian gospel and thereby bring the contemporary black church back to its linerating heritage. Our worship service must be free and liberating, because we believe "the Lord will make a way somehow." Therefore, we must fight until freedom comes.

The Theological Meaning of Black Worship

Black worship is more than an expression of our historical struggle to be free. Because it is more than what we do, a mere historical analysis of the context of its origin is simply not adequate. We can talk about certain sociological conditions and how they affected the style and content of our songs and sermons. We can mention slavery, the great migrations, the civil rights movement, and their effect on black worship. But we have not really touched the heart of black worship from the perspective of the people until we deal with the *theological* claim affirmed in prayer, song, and story.

In the struggle of black slaves to define their humanity according to freedom and not slavery there was present the divine Power who was greater than the white structures that enslaved them. When black slaves were tempted to give up in despair, this Power gave them hope that slavery would soon come to an end.

The source which black people used for explaining this Power was Scripture as interpreted by their African heritage and their desire for freedom. Black worship is biblical. One of the most amazing facts of history is that many African-American slaves did not accept the white interpretation of the gospel, even though they could not read or write. Although whites contended that Scripture endorsed slavery, black slaves argued differently. They contended that God willed their freedom and not their slavery. Their hermeneutics was not derived from an intellectual encounter with the text but from a gift of the Spirit. A white preacher in 1832 noted, "Many of the blacks look upon white people as merely taught by the Book; they consider themselves instructed by inspiration of the Spirit."[8]

Because slaves were able to make a radical epistemological distinction between the gospel of Jesus and the religion of whites, they also came to different theological conclusions about God. When African slaves heard the Old Testament story of Israel in Egypt, they identified themselves with the Hebrew slaves and identified white slaveholders with the Egyptians, and no amount of clever white exegesis could change their thinking on this matter. As Israel was in Egyptland, oppressed so hard they could not stand, so blacks were in American slavery, working under the whip and pistol. As Israel was liberated from Egypt across the Red Sea, so blacks would also be set free. It is this theological certainty that characterizes black worship, enabling blacks to sing with assurance:

> Oh Mary, don't you weep, don't you moan,
> Oh Mary, don't you weep, don't you moan,

8. Cited by Genovese in *Roll Jordan Roll*, p. 214.

> Pharaoh's army got drownded,
> Oh Mary, don't you weep.

The theme of God as the Liberator is found throughout the history of black religion. It is found among black Protestants and Catholics. Black Christians have always known that the God of the biblical tradition and of their African heritage is the One whose righteousness is identical with the liberation of the weak and helpless.

The theological conviction that the God of the Bible is the liberator of the poor and the downtrodden has been and is the important distinction between black and white religion. White Christianity may refer to liberation in limited times and places as shown by the abolitionists, the social gospel preachers, and the recent appearance of political and liberation theologians in Europe and America. But liberation is not and has never been the dominant theme in white church songs, prayers, and sermons. The reason is obvious: white people live in and identify with a social, economic, and political situation which blinds them to the biblical truth of liberation. Expecting white oppressors to recognize black liberation as central to the gospel is like expecting Pharaoh in Egypt to respond affirmatively to God's plea to "let my people go." To hear that plea is to recognize the limitations of one's power, a recognition oppressors seldom if ever make. Even when oppressors express the liberation theme in words, as found in Lyndon Johnson's affirmation that "we shall overcome" and white theologians' endorsement of liberation theology, that expression remains at a theoretical level and is seldom put into practice. White oppressors merely want to co-opt the language of the oppressed so they will not have to change societal structures of oppression.

In black religion and worship, God is known primarily as the liberator of the poor and the downtrodden. God is the Almighty Sovereign One who is sometimes called a "heartfixer" and a "mind regulator." During the worship service, God is known by the immediate presence of the divine Spirit with the people, giving them not only the vision that the society must be transformed but also the power and courage to participate in its transformation.

The certainty about God's immediate presence with the weak is the heart of the black worship service. Black worship is a series of recitals of what God has done to bring the people out of "hurt, harm, and danger." Through sermon, song, prayer, and testimony, the people tell their story of "how they got over." God is that divine miracle who enables the people to survive amid wretched conditions. God is holy, personal, and all-powerful. God is everything the people need in order to triumph over terrible circumstances.

It is important to note that there are no metaphysical distinctions between God and Jesus in black worship. The distinction between the Father and the Son is defined according to the rhythm of the people's language as they seek to communicate with the divine. Jesus is their constant companion, the one who walks with the people and tells them he is their own. He is the Oppressed One who experiences the brokenness of humanity. He is God's child who was born of "Sister Mary" in Bethlehem, and "everytime the baby cried, she'd a-rocked Him in the weary land."

In the black church, Jesus is also known for his identification with the poor, his suffering and death on the cross, and his resurrection from the dead. When the people get tired of struggling for survival and liberation and their "road gets rocky and rugged," they go to church in order to hear the preacher talk about Jesus. Sensing their impending despair, the preacher offers them hope by reminding them of the liberating power of Jesus' cross and resurrection:

> Have you considered the one who died on Calvary and was resurrected on the third day? Have you considered Jesus, the lily of the valley and the bright and morning star? He is able to smooth out the rough places in your life. He can place your feet on the solid rock of salvation.

It is not unusual for the preacher to call the name of Jesus repeatedly, according to the mood and spirit of the congregation. He may call Jesus' name as many as twenty-five or thirty times if the Spirit warrants it. If the people "get happy," as is so often the case, they may call Jesus' name for ten or fifteen minutes. In sermon, testimony, and prayer, the people invite Jesus to come and be with them and to "throw his strong arm of protection around them." To understand the theological significance of Jesus in black worship, the interpreter needs to experience Jesus' presence with the people and hear them call on his holy name as disclosed in this black deacon's prayer:

Uh Jesus, we know all power is in thy hands. Uh Jesus! Uh Jesus! We need you right now. Uh Jesus, I know you heard me pray in days that's past and gone. Don't turn a deaf ear to thy servant's prayer right now. Uh Jesus, Uh Jesus![9]

The importance of Jesus and God in the black church service is perhaps best explained when one considers the preponderance of suffering in black life. When we consider slavery, lynching, and ghettos, how can we explain black people's mental and physical survival? How was it possible for black slaves to hope for freedom when a mere empirical analysis of their situation of oppression would elicit despair? How is it possible for poor blacks today to keep their sanity in the struggle for freedom when one considers the continued worsening of their economic exploitation? The answer is found in Jesus and God. Jesus heals wounded spirits and broken hearts. No matter what trials and tribulations the people encounter, they refuse to let despair define their humanity. They simply believe that "God can make a way out of no way." Blacks do not deny that trouble is present in their life; they merely contend that trouble does not have the last word, and that "we'll understand it better by and by." In the words of Charles Tindley,

Trials dark on every hand, and we cannot understand.
All the ways that God would lead us to that Blessed Promise Land.
But God guides us with God's eye and we'll follow till we die.
For we'll understand it better by and by.

By and by, when the morning comes,
All the saints of God are gathered home.
We'll tell the story how we overcome.
For we'll understand it better by and by.

---

9. Cited by Harold A. Carter in *The Prayer Tradition of Black People* (Valley Forge, Pa.: Judson Press, 1976), p. 49.

Black Ecumenism and the
Liberation Struggle

THE THEME "BLACK ECUMENISM AND THE LIBERATION STRUGGLE" IS important, because it connects the movement for unity among the churches with the struggle for freedom in the larger society. When the World Council of Churches was formed in Amsterdam in 1948, the term *ecumenical* had acquired a modern meaning that referred to "the relations between and unity of two or more churches (or of Christians of various confessions)."[1] This definition remained dominant in theological and church contexts until the recent appearance of highly articulate and radical theological voices from Asia, Latin America, and Africa and its diaspora. Third World theologians began to insist on a definition of ecumenism that moved beyond the traditional interconfessional issues to the problems of poverty and the struggle for social and economic justice in a global context. In their attempt to connect ecumenism with the economic and political struggle for a fuller human life for all, Third World theologians also began to uncover the original and more comprehensive meaning of the term *oikoumene*. In the Greco-Roman world generally and also in the New Testament, *oikoumene* referred to the whole inhabited world and not simply religious activities.[2] With this broader perspective in mind, it is appropriate to apply the term *ecumenical* to "both secular and religious aspirations toward achieving a united

1. W. A. Visser 't Hooft, "The Word 'Ecumenical'—Its History and Use," in *A History of the Ecumenical Movement, 1517-1948,* ed. Ruth Rouse and S. C. Neill (London: SPCK, 1967), p. 735.
2. See Visser 't Hooft, "The Word 'Ecumenical'—Its History and Use," p. 735.

This paper was originally presented at a conference entitled "Black Ecumenism and the Liberation Struggle" held at Yale University on 16-17 February 1978. It was also presented at the Quinn Chapel African Methodist Episcopal Church on the occasion of their 131st anniversary, 22 May 1978. It was published in *The Journal of the Interdenominational Center* 7 (Fall 1979): 1-10.

human family living in harmony with its global habitat."[3] In this essay, I will examine the meaning of black ecumenism in the context of black people's struggle for freedom.

Black Ecumenism and the White Church

The phrase "black ecumenism" is significant because black churches have traditionally resisted in the limitation of the term *ecumenical* to the unity among churches. Black church people contend that the search for unity in Jesus Christ cannot be separated from the struggle for justice in society. While black independent churches may have derived their names as well as credal statements from white churches, it is not correct to say that black churches were created purely for *sociological* reasons.[4] If we take seriously the contention of the sociologists of knowledge that all ideas (including theological ones) are dialectically related to social reality, then it is also true that black people's separation from white churches was a social protest grounded in their *theological* affirmation that the God of Jesus cannot tolerate segregation in the church or the society. Segregation in the white churches prompted black people to organize independent churches that would be committed to preaching and living the gospel of freedom. Segregation and slavery in the society prompted black churches to define black people's political resistance against oppression as a witness to God's eschatological intentions to estab-

3. This definition is given by Margaret Nash at the beginning of her book *Ecumenical Movement in the 1960's* (Johannesburg: Raven Press, 1975). This book offers a good account of the impact of Asian, African, and Latin American churches upon the World Council of Churches. See also W. A. Visser 't Hooft, *Has the Ecumenical Movement a Future?* (Belfast: Christian Journals Limited, 1974), and his "The General Ecumenical Development since 1948" in *The Ecumenical Advance: A History of the Ecumenical Movement, 1948-1968*, vol. 2, ed. Harold Fey (London: SPCK, 1970).

4. Both black and white scholars have often reduced the appearance of the autonomous black churches during the nineteenth century to social factors and to the exclusion of theology. See, for example, H. Richard Niebuhr in *The Social Sources of Denominationalism* (Cleveland: World Publishing, 1929): "The causes of the racial schism are not difficult to determine. Neither theology nor polity furnished the occasion for it. The sole source of this denominationalism is social." Even J. Deotis Roberts can write that "We left the white churches for non-theological reasons" ("A Black Ecclesiology of Involvement," *Journal of Religious Thought* 32 [Spring-Summer 1975]: 43). Another example of this error can be found in Joseph Washington's *Black Religion* (Boston: Beacon, 1964).

lish justice for the poor and weak in the land. Whether we speak of northern black independent churches, of blacks who remained in white churches, or of the so-called "invisible institution" in the South, the dominant theme in black ecclesiology is God's election and empowerment of an oppressed community to struggle for justice in human society. Northern black church people such as Henry Garnet and David Walker were bold in their affirmation of divine righteousness against the evils of segregation and slavery. Walker's "Appeal" (1829) and Garnet's "Address to the Slaves of the United States of America" (1843) are theological manifestoes that remind us of the chasm that existed between black religion and white religion, even when they were practiced in the same denominations.[5]

While "free" northern blacks such as Garnet and Walker expressed their views about the justice of God openly, southern black slaves were normally not permitted to worship separately unless authorized white people were present to proctor the meeting. In order to escape the limitations of white religion, black slaves held secret worship services that later historians have referred to as the "invisible institution." When it was not possible for slaves to "steal away" into the woods at night, they often camouflaged their language with biblical and apocalyptic images. A fugitive slave from North Carolina reminded a post–Civil War black congregation how "we used to have to employ our dark symbols and obscure figures to cover our real meaning."[6] The possibility of hidden and militant meanings in the slave songs has prompted much debate over their precise meaning by later interpreters. But whether we claim that the slave spirituals were primarily this-worldly, political, or spiritual in essence, one fact is clear: a militant and political reading is always possible for anyone who connects these songs with the universal claim of the gospel message. Apparently harmless songs can become revolutionary affirmations if there is already present the seed of revolution among the oppressed. In a slave situation where whites were given inordinate privileges, blacks could use their songs to express God's judgment against slavery as well as their own political intentions to fight for freedom.

5. Walker's "Appeal" and Garnet's "Address" are reprinted together in *Walker's "Appeal" and Garnet's "Address to the Slaves of the United States of America,"* American Negro: His History and Literature Series (New York: Arno Press, 1969).

6. Cited by Donald G. Matthews in *Religion in the Old South* (Chicago: University of Chicago Press, 1977), p. 218.

> Ev'body got to rise to meet King Jesus in th' morning
> Th' high and th' low
> th' rich and th' po'
> Th' bond and th' free
> As well as me.

Sometimes, however, slaves openly expressed their rejection of the white church and its theology. "God never made us to be slaves for white people," a maid boldly asserted to her mistress.[7] Because blacks believed that "God is no respecter of persons" (Acts 10:34, KJV), they seldom regarded the white church as a true representative of the body of Christ. "When a group in one autonomous black church threatened to leave the congregation because of the minister's 'scandalous' behavior, he taunted them for running to the whites. If you want to 'sit by the door when the white folks have communion, an' wait there 'til they get through 'fore you get some. *Come now,* an' get your letter!'"[8]

The theme of God's impartiality is not only found in black churches of the nineteenth century but also in the twentieth century. In the writings of such black theologians as Howard Thurman and Benjamin Mays, and in the political activism of Adam Clayton Powell, Jr., and Martin Luther King, Jr., the black church projected an image of church unity based on a political commitment of justice for the poor. The absence of any serious commitment of white Christians to eliminate racism in their churches and in the society accounts for the lack of serious dialogue on the part of black independent churches in the ecumenical deliberations of the Consultation on Church Union, the National Council of Churches, and the World Council of Churches in Geneva. We blacks do not believe that church unity with white people is meaningful unless it arises out of a demonstrated commitment to implement justice in the society. Willie White, a Baptist preacher, is even more emphatic:

> It is precisely God's purpose that stands opposed to any thoroughgoing ecumenical approach between the black and white churches of America. . . . For the establishment of the black church was not the work of a mere man; it was the work of Christ. . . . [Its] task [therefore] is to stand everywhere in the world as a Christian symbol of God's opposition to oppression.

---

7. Cited by Matthews in *Religion in the Old South*, p. 221.
8. Matthews, *Religion in the Old South*, p. 211.

White [people] must be made to realize that the black church is the instrument of God, in this world, not just a group of nigger churchgoers who are separated unto themselves until the good graces of white [people] call them back into fellowship with white congregations.[9]

Although representatives of the black church attend ecumenical gatherings and hear lectures on the unity of the church by well-known Protestant and Catholic theologians, black participants soon realize that there is a huge gap between theological doctrines about the church and the actual practice of white church people. It is therefore hard not to conclude that white theologians are supported by their churches in order to reconcile the irreconcilable—namely, white domination and the gospel of Jesus. How else can we explain all their talk about our unity in the body of Christ when they have no intentions of removing the barriers that separate us? My first extensive experience with this peculiar white attitude that calls itself "Christian" began at Garrett Theological Seminary and was later reinforced by white preachers involved in the civil rights movement. When I was at Garrett (from 1958 to 1963), black students could not understand why most of our teachers and white classmates remained conspicuously silent about black people's struggle for justice in American society. It was as if whites believed that the Bible, theology, and the church had nothing to do with life.

Later, after my graduation from seminary, I encountered a similar contradiction as the white churches of North America failed to come to terms with the theological significance of the civil rights movement. One of the most blatant examples of this contradiction was the appeal of eight white ministers of Birmingham who denounced Martin Luther King, Jr., and urged "our own Negro Community to withdraw support" because the demonstrations were "untimely and unwise." King responded with his now-famous "Letter from Birmingham Jail."[10] King's dialogue with white church people disclosed not only how far he was willing to go in order to achieve a genuine reconciliation between blacks and whites but also the limitations of a white

9. White, "Ecumenism and the Black Church," *Christian Century*, 13 February 1974, p. 179.

10. See the "Letter from Birmingham Jail" in King's *Why We Can't Wait* (New York: Signet, 1963), pp. 76-95.

perspective in the context of a black liberation struggle. As we black Christians listened to white theological rhetoric about the justice of God and the unity of the church and then related it to white passivity regarding the transformation of ecclesiastical and social structures of oppression, we could not help but conclude that white church people talk about love and reconciliation but seldom with the practical intention of translating theological doctrines into political realities. The rise of black theology was partly due to the need to unmask this white theological hypocrisy so that black people would not be deceived by carefully structured theological ideas that were unrelated to their struggle for justice.

Black Ecumenism and the Rise of Black Theology

Is the ecumenical significance of black theology limited to the need for uncovering the hypocrisy of white Christians? I think not. The theme of "black ecumenism and the liberation struggle" also challenges contemporary black denominational churches to implement in society the freedom they sing and preach about in worship. One of the constant dangers facing oppressed people is the temptation to imitate their oppressors, even when the two groups remain socially separate. During the time of slavery and the rigid segregation that followed the reconstruction, the lines between the black and the white, the poor and the rich, were clearly drawn, and there were many black churches who took their stand on the side of oppressed blacks in their fight for justice. The political solidarity of the black churches with the poor was characteristic of their involvement in the civil rights movement, and this political struggle united Baptists, Methodists, Presbyterians, Pentecostals, and Catholics. The institutional expression of the ecumenism among black Christians appeared with the formation of the National Committee of Negro Churchmen, which is now called the National Conference of Black Christians (NCBC). NCBC was a politically active group of ecumenical church people who took seriously Willie White's contention that black Christians

> must realize that the Baptist Articles of Faith and other such statements have nothing to do with the definition of the black church. The black church is defined by the very ideas which demand a new ecumenism among black Christians . . . not by

any or all of the traditionally accepted creeds but by the creed of
liberation: the creed that one [person] does not have the right
to oppress another, be the other black or white, baptized by
immersion or by sprinkling, fashionably attired or running
naked in the jungle. It is defined by the creed that the dehumanization of one [person] by another is in total contradiction to the way of Christ and must be opposed. And it is this
creed that makes possible the . . . black church community.[11]

Is this definition of black ecumenism still a dominant expression of the faith of independent black church denominations? Do black churches, as institutions, still regard black
people's struggle for political liberation as the theological foundation of their *raison d'être*? If black church people would answer
these questions in the affirmative, then all I can say is that their
judgment about themselves differs significantly from many black
non-Christians who at best regard the churches as irrelevant in
the black struggle for justice. Aside from two or three isolated
examples, where is the empirical evidence that black churches are
involved in the liberation struggle of the poor? How long will we
continue to appeal to the black heroes of the past as evidence for
the contemporary relevance of the black church?

My questions are not intended as a theological put-down of the
black church, because I have been a minister in the African Methodist Episcopal Church since I was sixteen years old. Anyone
acquainted with my theological perspective knows that I believe
that Christian theology has its validity only insofar as it arises out
of and is accountable to the church of Jesus Christ. Indeed, it is
because of my commitment to the black church that I must ask
whether some black congregations—or entire denominations—
do not act so as to require us to make the theological judgment
that they are no longer the church of Jesus Christ. If the church's
mission is to serve suffering humanity and not itself, can we really
say that the black church of today lives the faith that it proclaims?

These are difficult questions, and they cannot be answered for
all churches in the same way. Some are more faithful than others.
But if we are serious about black ecumenism and the liberation
struggle, then we had better not sidestep the apostasy of the black
church. To be sure, the black church looks good when compared
with the sick history of the white church. But what about our

11. White, "Ecumenism and the Black Church," p. 180.

relations with our brothers and sisters who believe that black churches are destructive forces in the struggle for political freedom? We may rightly claim that our separation from the white church is due to white racism, but what is the reason for continued separation from *each other?* How can we bridge the gap between the African Methodist Episcopal, African Methodist Episcopal Zion, and Christian Methodist Episcopal Churches so that they can become united in the struggle for freedom? How can we remove the barriers that separate Baptists and Pentecostals, Catholics and Anglicans, and a host of other assorted black church people? Since many outsiders view our separation as indicative of institutional self-interest, it is necessary for us to state the *theological* reasons for our separation. What is the relation between our institutional life and the gospel which our institutions claim to serve? How important are our denominational identities in our definition of the gospel, especially since most of the names of our churches are derived from white denominations?

It seems that black denominations today are not good models of black ecumenism. With the decline in the black churches' support for NCBC, black Christians do not appear to be united in Christ for the purpose of liberating suffering humanity. Black churches seem content with preaching sermons and singing songs about freedom, but few of them have made an institutional commitment to organize church life and work for the creation of freedom.

During the civil rights movement and other high points of black ecumenism, the unity of the black churches was found in a religious expression grounded in the practice of freedom in the larger society. When our faith in God was expressed in the struggle for justice, we were joined together by a common spirit of liberation that controlled our community. When that common commitment to the struggle for liberation is gone, as with many black churches today, then the gospel becomes identified with the maintenance of a particular denominational structure. Some black Christians begin to think that to be Christian is to be Methodist or Baptist, as if our identity in Christ is defined by the historical and religious experiences of John Wesley and Roger Williams.

The confusion about ecumenism and liberation in the black church is also found in its attitude toward the relationship be-

tween men and women. The black church, like all all other
churches, is a male-dominated church. The difficulty that black
male ministers have in supporting the equality of women in the
church and society stems partly from the lack of a clear liberation
criterion rooted in the gospel and in the present struggles of
oppressed peoples. In many contexts the black church is as back-
ward and obscene on the issue of sexism as is the white church. It
is truly amazing that many black male ministers, young and old,
can hear the message of liberation in the gospel when related to
racism but remain deaf to a similar message in the context of
sexism. As Frances Beale says, the black man "sees the system for
what it really is for the most part, but where he rejects its values
and mores on many issues, when it comes to women, he seems to
take his guidelines from the pages of the *Ladies Home Journal.*"[12]
How can we be so radical when viewing the liberation of black
male ministers from white domination and then be so conservative about the pains of our black sisters? If our concept of black
ecumenism does not include our struggle to give equal status to
women in the church and the society, then it is not Christian.
Christian freedom is contagious. Its very nature requires that it
be given to all—white and black, male and female. When the
black church is evaluated by this theological criterion, the gap
between the theory of freedom and the practice of freedom becomes blatantly obvious.

If the black church denominations could begin to deal creatively with the problems of separation among themselves as well
as with sexism in the churches, they would be in a better position
to deal with the problems of unity between black Christians and
non-Christians. Among the old and young alike, black churches
have serious credibility problems, because there are so many of
them that appear to be indifferent to the poor and weak. To be
sure, we can continue to refer to past heroes and martyrs, but in
what way does the contemporary black church continue that tradition? As I look around the present black church scene and
evaluate where it uses its economic and political resources, I think
it is very difficult to show any institutional commitment to the
freedom of people from societal oppression. The black church
seems to be concerned about serving only itself. While it still

12. Beale, "Double Jeopardy: To Be Black and Female" in *The Black Woman*,
ed. Toni Cade (New York: Signet, 1970), p. 92.

preaches sermons and sings songs about freedom, its claims about freedom are not incorporated into a social theory that will assist in the implementation of freedom. It is the absence of any carefully worked out social theory for the implementation of our religious confessions that makes black non-Christians suspicious of churchly intentions. Black ecumenism therefore must be broad enough to include all black people who strive for freedom or we have no grounds for connecting it with the theme of liberation. The theme of political liberation extends black ecumenism beyond confessional unity and affirms a oneness based on a practical solidarity with the poor. We begin to realize what Malcolm X taught us:

> When we come together, we don't come together as Baptists or Methodists. You don't catch hell because you are a Baptist, and you don't catch hell because you're a Methodist . . . , you don't catch hell because you're a Democrat or a Republican, you don't catch hell because you're a Mason or an Elk, and you sure don't catch hell because you're an American; because if you were an American, you wouldn't catch hell. You catch hell because you're a black [person]. You catch hell, all of us catch hell for the same reason.[13]

In this quotation, Malcolm has identified a major contradiction in American culture—racism. Since black churches came into being as a protest against racism, it is unfortunate that many black church people cling rigidly to white denominational labels that were and are responsible for our separation. As long as we are divided on the basis of confessional expressions of faith that were not created in our historical experience, black church people will continue to have difficulties in relating the confession of faith and the struggle for freedom.

The same theological distortion that separates black churches among themselves, separates men and women, and separates black non-Christians and Christians in North America also accounts for the present failures of black church mission in Africa and other Third World countries. For example, do Africans think that North American black missionaries and bishops from the African Methodist Episcopal, African Methodist Episcopal Zion, or Baptist Churches are more responsive to the African

13. Malcolm X, *Malcolm X Speaks* (New York: Grove Press, 1966), p. 4.

liberation struggle than white missionaries? Every African that I have talked with answered this question by saying that there is little difference between black and white missionaries, except in skin color. With so much talk about Africanization, indigenization, and the selfhood of the African churches, why are black denominations so slow in their support of a truly independent African church? Members of the African Methodist Episcopal and African Methodist Episcopal Zion Churches have been in Africa nearly a century, and both churches still send black North American bishops as leaders in Africa rather than developing an indigenous leadership among Africans. The African Methodist Episcopal Church has elected only two indigenous Africans as bishops for service in Africa—Francis Gow (1956) and Harold B. Senatle (1984)—and the African Methodist Episcopal Zion Church has elected only one—Solomon D. Lartey (1960). What does that tell us about their commitment to an independent African theology and church? Furthermore, the black American bishops assigned to Africa are not chosen because of their particular interest or expertise in African life, but because of internal church politics—namely, the seniority system. The most recently elected bishops are usually sent to Africa because it is the least desirable place to be if one intends to be influential in shaping church policy. The fact that the African mission is controlled by the interests of North American black church people is a disgrace to the legacy of Henry M. Turner, not to mention the gospel of Jesus Christ.

Of course, my critique of black churches in relation to their African mission is not intended to suggest that they have done no creative work on this continent of Africa. Indeed, African Methodist Episcopal Bishop H. H. Brookins's support of the freedom fighters in Zimbabwe is an important reminder that Bishop Henry M. Turner has not been forgotten. I am sure that there are other prominent examples that could be mentioned. In fact, it is because of the significant exceptions that I am forced to ask why we don't structure the black church in such a way that it will become a visible instrument of African liberation. If we are serious about our African identity, as the names of some of our church denominations suggest, why not embody it in a historical commitment on behalf of our brothers and sisters in Africa? Our ability to implement this concern in the structures of our churches will show how serious we are about black ecumenism.

The same credibility problem that the black church encounters in Africa also exists in Asia and Latin America. To church people in Asia and Latin America, the black church in North America seems to be a colored version of the white church. Both the white and black churches seem to be content with an economic system of capitalism that is so dehumanizing to the vast majority of human beings in the world. To be sure, black churches have been critical of the lack of justice for black people in North American society. But where is the black church's social critique in the global context in which the vast majority of humanity suffers? If we do not place our claims for justice in a global context, then we will appear to Asians, Africans, and Latin Americans to be black capitalists who are upset only because we have not been given a larger piece of the American pie. What does the black church have to say about the fact that more than two-thirds of the world's population exists in poverty and that such material conditions are directly traceable to the exploitation of poor countries by rich ones? The United States represents six percent of the world's population but consumes forty percent of the world's resources. When we black people speak of justice, do we mean that we want equal share of the forty percent? If that is what we mean, then there is very little difference between black people and white people in the United States when they are evaluated from the viewpoint of global justice. If we think that the theological difference between the black church and white church is visible even in an international context, then we need to articulate that difference in theory and in practice so that poor people in Asia, Africa, and Latin America will recognize the nature of our difference. Aside from a few symbolic gestures in relation to Africa and the Caribbean, black church people have not shown that they view their civil rights struggle as a radical challenge to the evils of capitalism and as a historical expression of their solidarity with the poor people of the world. I believe that the time has come for the black church to display a form of black ecumenism that arises out of our historical commitment to defend the cause of the poor in the world. The poor must include not only black Americans but also Africans, Asians, and Latin Americans. What would black ecumenism look like if the black church accepted the challenge to define the body of Christ according to a people's commitment to liberate the oppressed of the world? If we believe that the gospel we preach is universal and therefore intended for all peoples, are we not required to express this universality in our service to all humankind?

The ecumenical perspective that connects the unity of humankind with the liberation of the world's poor does not diminish our focus on *black* liberation. Rather, it enhances it, not only because the vast majority of the world's poor are colored but also because economic exploitation is a disease that requires the cooperation of all victims if the world is to be transformed. The vocation of the poor is to struggle together for the transformation of their history. Their struggle to transform the world according to the Christian vision as disclosed in the cross and resurrection of Jesus makes known to them that "unity only becomes a reality to the extent that we partake of Christ (who) is hidden in those who suffer."[14]

14. Rubem Alves, "Protestantism in Latin America: Its Ideological Function and Utopian Possibilities," *The Ecumenical Review,* January 1970, p. 15.

Postscript

NO EXPERIENCE OUTSIDE OF THE UNITED STATES HAS HAD A DEEPER impact upon my theological perspective than my recent visit to South Africa. The concluding essay, "A Black American's Perspective on South Africa," represents my initial reflections on that visit. To speak the truth about South Africa involves great risks of life and imprisonment, especially if one is a resident of that country. That is why so few white South Africans speak the truth about that land. But apartheid is so inhuman to black South Africans that many have come to believe that speaking the truth is no longer a choice but a necessity that arises from being human and Christian. So they continue to resist apartheid, because they believe what the Reverend Henry Highland Garnet said to black slaves in 1843: "Liberty is a spirit sent from God, and like its great Author, is no respector of persons."

A Black American's Perspective on South Africa

MY FIRST CONTACT WITH BLACK CHRISTIANS IN SOUTH AFRICA OCcurred in early 1971, when I received a letter from the organizers of the newly formed Black Theology Project of the University Christian Movement requesting me to send a tape of one of my lectures on black theology for a seminar in Johannesburg. I was greatly surprised by the request but very pleased that black theology was being talked about and discussed in South Africa. I sent a tape entitled "Christ in Black Theology," the fifth chapter of my newly published text *A Black Theology of Liberation* (1970). About a month later, I received a telegram requesting another copy of the tape. I found out later from South Africans visiting Union Seminary and from a newsletter of the South African Student's Association (SASO) that the first tape had been confiscated in a police raid of the headquarters of the University Christian Movement.

From the papers presented in a series of seminars held across the country in 1971 there emerged the first book on black theology in South Africa, entitled *Essays on Black Theology* (1972). The contributions included "Black Consciousness and the Quest for a True Humanity" by Steve Biko, the first president of SASO, who was subsequently murdered by the South African police; "An African Theology or a Black Theology" by Manas Buthelezi, one of the influential initiators of the development of black theology in South Africa and now a Lutheran bishop; "Corporate Personality in Israel and in Africa" by Bonganjalo Goba, a graduate of Chicago Theological Seminary and currently a professor in the department of ethics at the University of South Africa; and "Black Theology and Authority" by Mokgethi Motlhabi, a graduate of Boston University and author of *The Theory and Practice of Black Resistance to Apartheid* (1985). I also contributed an essay entitled "Black Theology and Black Liberation."

As one might expect, *Essays on Black Theology* was banned im-

mediately by the South African government, along with the Black
Theology Project and its parent organization, the University
Christian Movement. Many South African black theologians
were also banned and imprisoned. The black theology movement
had to go underground. I was kept informed about the happen-
ings in South Africa by many students and church leaders whom I
met in international conferences and also at Union Seminary. I
met Desmond Tutu for the first time at Union at a conference on
African and black theologies in 1973, and I met Alan Boesak as a
visiting student at Union and Colgate-Rochester Divinity Schools
doing research on Martin Luther King, Jr., Malcolm X, and black
theology in 1974.

Before my July 1985 trip to South Africa, I made two previous
attempts to enter that country. My first application for a visa was
denied with no explanation given. I made a second attempt in
1976, when I was invited by the South African Council of
Churches (SACC) to attend a meeting of church leaders in Johannesburg. To my surprise, I was issued a visa. However, when I
arrived in Geneva for a brief stopover at the World Council of
Churches headquarters, the South African Consul-General in
Geneva gave me the following message, first by telephone and
later in a hand-delivered note:

> Inasmuch as the Chief Magistrate of Pretoria has declined to
> give his permission for the holding of the Hammanskraal semi-
> nar, scheduled for 9 to 13 August 1976, the Department of the
> Interior desired you to be informed that your visa to visit South
> Africa, which was issued solely for the purpose of enabling you
> to attend the seminar, is no longer valid and should be re-
> garded as withdrawn. If you should in any event decide to come
> to South Africa, it would unfortunately not be possible to admit
> you.

After two unsuccessful attempts to enter the Republic of South
Africa, I concluded that I would never be permitted to enter that
country so long as its white dictatorship held power. Then in
March of 1985 I received a letter from the United States–South
Africa Leader Exchange Program (USSALEP, founded in 1958
as a charitable educational association) inviting me to join with a
group of South African theologians and church leaders to participate in a three-year study of the role of the church in the changing society of South Africa. I had never heard of USSALEP. But

the names of several people participating in the study or indirectly related to it gave it impeccable credibility: Beyers Naudé, general secretary of SACC; Desmond Tutu and Alan Boesak; Takatso Mofokeng, author of *The Crucified among the Crossbearers: Towards a Black Christology* (1983); John W. de Gruchy, author of *The Church Struggle in South Africa* (1979); and Charles Villa-Vicencio, editor with de Gruchy of *Apartheid Is a Heresy* (1983). I was also informed that my former colleague Cornel West of Yale was being invited to participate in the study. I immediately accepted the invitation, although I still assumed that I would never be given a visa to enter South Africa.

Shortly after I received the USSALEP invitation, I was informed that a South African edition of my book *For My People* (1984) had been issued by Skotaville, a black publishing company in that country. With the knowledge that several of my books had already been banned, and with the belief that a similar fate awaited *For My People*, I found it difficult to prepare for my departure. As the time approached, I could not get out of my mind the idea that I would receive word (at the last minute, of course) that my visa application had been rejected. Even after I received a visa in late June, I still believed that it would be withdrawn before my departure date.

When Cornel West and I departed for South Africa on 7 July 1985, we discussed the probability of being turned back at the airport in Johannesburg. Since I had had the experience of having my visa withdrawn while en route, I knew that having it stamped in my passport did not guarantee that I would be permitted to enter the country. We arrived around 10:30 A.M. As we deplaned and proceeded to walk toward the passport controls, I said to West that I did not believe we would be allowed to enter the country. His response reinforced my sentiments.

When I presented my passport to the passport controls officer, he welcomed me to South Africa with a smile and wished me a pleasant stay in the country. Then, after a few seconds, his facial expression changed slightly, indicating that he had found something about me that disturbed him. He pushed a button and four officials joined him as they discussed my situation among themselves in Afrikaans. After a few minutes, they asked me to take a seat. When I inquired about the nature of the problem, the official said, "These things happen sometimes. Just take a seat, and I will call you shortly." Cornel West was given a similar message.

We waited about two hours before Dr. Michael Sinclair, the executive director of USSALEP, appeared and informed us that we could now proceed through the passport controls. As we collected our bags, everyone was courteous, expressing their regrets for any inconvenience the delay may have caused.

As we walked through the airport toward the car, an eerie feeling engulfed me. "I can't believe that I am in South Africa," I thought to myself, "the land of apartheid and the black struggle against it. What will I do if an Afrikaner attacks me or if a policeman arrests me? Suppose I am taken to one of those infamous prisons where so many black South Africans have been tortured and killed." I thought of what Mississippi and Alabama symbolized in the black struggle for civil rights during the 1950s and '60s.

Fear for my physical safety quickly subsided, but a much more important concern soon overwhelmed me. "What will this experience mean for my theological vocation, for my struggle to understand the meaning of the gospel today?" No human being can encounter a horrendous evil like apartheid and then walk away unaffected by it. Though not sure in what way, I knew that my theological perspective would be deeply affected by the South African reality.

When one arrives in South Africa, the first impressions can be deceptive. Johannesburg has the appearance of a modern Western city; it reminded me of a city in southern California. But, appearances to the contrary, there are great differences. Perceptive observers will soon enough note the conspicuous presence of blacks as servants of whites—whites who give little evidence of treating blacks any differently than masters treat their animals. Since I grew up in the southern part of the United States and was always taught at home, church, and school to hate racism, a surge of suppressed feelings of resentment gushed to the surface of my consciousness as I observed the racist attitudes of white South Africans treating blacks as if "they have no rights which whites were bound to respect."

I resisted the urge to express my anger, because I wanted to know more about the Afrikaners' mind. I wanted to talk to them about their belief that apartheid is God's will and then compare my findings with what I knew about white segregationists I grew up with in the South. But even more important, I wanted to meet my black brothers and sisters in Soweto, Durban, and Cape Town and find out more about their theological reflections on black resistance and the spirituality that sustains it. What was it that empowered their children to fight heavily armed police with sticks and stones?

Our first meeting was with Beyers Naudé and Takatso Mofokeng, a South African member of our team now teaching theology at the University of Botswana. We discussed strategy and were given a quick overview of the state of the churches and society in South Africa. It was my first encounter with Naudé, the rejected leader of the Afrikaner community. He is a man of much wisdom and humility who is possessed with an unshakable determination to fight for a just South Africa. I was equally impressed with Mofokeng, who has a brilliant theological mind and is deeply committed to the freedom of his people.

Mofokeng, West, and I constituted the team that was commissioned to take a quick survey of religious and other leaders in the black and white communities of South Africa for the purpose of evaluating the role that the churches should and could play in the current crisis in the country. We listened to the views of different groups and put critical questions to all. We traveled from Johannesburg to Cape Town and talked to blacks as well as whites (including many Afrikaner theologians and church leaders) about apartheid in the society and the role of the churches in relation to it. Whether liberal or conservative, the comments of blacks and whites differed significantly. White liberals expressed a feeling that there was a strong need for change, but they seemed very pessimistic about a creative possibility for it. Afrikaners claimed to see little need for change and often seemed puzzled that anyone desired it. Blacks seemed possessed by a determined will to be free "by any means necessary." While acknowledging the odds against them, they appeared to be driven by a Spirit greater than themselves. They exhibited a hope that could not be shattered by the brutality of the South African police. All the blacks (and a few whites with whom we spoke) contended that radical change was inevitable because, as they said in their "Kairos Document," "the time has come. The moment of truth has arrived."

Our schedule involved discussions with black theologians in Soweto, the staff of the SACC, several theologians and church leaders of the Dutch Reformed Church (Nederduitse Gereformeerde Kerk), black theologians at the Institute of Contextual

Theology, the theology faculties of the University of South Africa and the University of Potchefstroom, community and church leaders in Durban, faculty and students at the Federal Seminary in Pietermaritzburg, and some representatives of the Azanian People's Organization (AZAPO, a black nationalist organization strongly influenced by the thinking of Steve Biko). We concluded our visit with a trip to Cape Town, where we spent three days meeting with church leaders, visiting the Crossroads squatter community, talking with the faculty of theology at the University of Western Cape, and finally reviewing our findings with the full team of South African theologians.

The climax of our visit to Cape Town included attendance at the memorial service for Fort Calate, Sicelo Mahlawuli, Sparrow Mkhonto, and Mathew Goniwe, four United Democratic Front (UDF) leaders who were assassinated in their efforts to establish a just South Africa. Everyone with whom I spoke regarded them as victims of the state rather than of the differences in philosophy and strategy between AZAPO and UDF.

The service began with the singing of "Kumba-yah My Lord." I have heard this song many times, but never like I heard it on that day. Perhaps the difference was the occasion and what South Africa has now come to mean to me existentially. When the congregation sang

> Someone dying, Lord, Kumba-yah,
> Oh, Lord, Kumba-yah

I could feel the power of God's presence in our midst. Some persons were crying and others were praying. All were searching for meaning in the death of these young men.

Alan Boesak was the preacher. I have heard few people who can speak the truth of the gospel with the integrity and power exemplified in the life and sermons of Alan Boesak. He stood in that pulpit as a person possessed by the truth of the gospel, challenging the South African government as the prophets of biblical religion had confronted Israelite kings and as Martin Luther King, Jr., had demanded that the U.S. government stop its war in Vietnam. As I sat there listening to Boesak speak from the depth of his faith, telling the people assembled "we shall overcome" and "don't get weary," because "there is a great camp meeting in the promised land," I could feel the surge of a mighty hope arise in their being. When Boesak proclaimed love instead of hate, hope instead of despair, that message bestowed upon the people not passivity but a greater spirit of resistance.

I could not help but think about black people's struggle in the United States, especially during the civil rights movement, as we comforted the wounded and buried our dead but refused to allow the deeds of evil people to destroy our determination to be free. We just kept on singing "I'm on My Way to Freedom Land" and "Ain't Gonna Let Nobody Turn Me Around." In black history, no one expressed this hope with greater clarity and depth than Martin Luther King, Jr. "I'm not going to stop singing 'We Shall Overcome,'" he often said,

> because I know that "truth crushed to the earth shall rise again." I am not going to stop singing "We Shall Overcome," because I know the Bible is right, "you shall reap what you sow." I am not going to stop singing "We Shall Overcome," because I know that one day the God of the universe will say to those who won't listen to him, "I'm not a playboy. Don't play with me. For I will rise up and break the backbone of your power." I'm not going to stop singing "We Shall Overcome," because "mine eyes have seen the glory of the coming of the Lord. He's trampling out the vintage where the grapes of wrath are stored. Glory hallelujah, his truth is marching on."

In South Africa, Alan Boesak, Desmond Tutu, and a host of others are preaching a similar hope. Most left the memorial service with a renewed determination to continue the fight for a just South Africa, knowing that the God of biblical religion is one whose righteousness is revealed in the empowerment of the weak.

At the end of my short stay, several things became very clear to me.

1. White South Africans, particularly Afrikaners, are determined to keep apartheid intact with only surface changes at best. "Separate development," the sophisticated way of talking about apartheid, is so deeply ingrained in the religion and culture of whites that many seem surprised that clear-thinking people do not share their views. To be sure, some will acknowledge that they have made some mistakes and that some changes are needed to improve the situation of blacks. But the great majority of whites believe that progress is taking place and that the present unrest will soon be over if outside agitators will permit South Africa to

solve its own problems. They believe that South Africa has gotten "bad" press coverage from foreign newspeople and from "self-appointed" leaders such as Boesak and Tutu. According to their reading of the Bible, God has ordained separate development and so it must be in the best interests of all, including blacks.

It is one thing to read about people who say such things, but it is another to sit face to face with whites who say them, expecting blacks in the group to agree with them. When I heard this sort of thing the first time, I was deeply shocked and disturbed and had to reach deep into the resources of my being in order to keep my cool. I asked God for strength to restrain my anger and patience to listen in the midst of this difficult and very uncomfortable situation. I really wanted to observe the Afrikaner's mind-set at work so as to figure out its essential character.

It did not take me long to understand the reasoning of Afrikaners. It is quite similar to the reasoning of the southern whites I encountered during my childhood and the civil rights movement, although there are obvious important differences between them. One factor which partly accounts for the great differences between southern whites and Afrikaners is the absence of the North and the liberal democratic tradition of freedom and equality that is deeply embedded in American history. Afrikaners have no such tradition of freedom which they apply to blacks. Its absence in politics and religion has meant that whites have been able not only to deny the humanity of blacks in the laws that define human relations but to do so without significant objections from any segment of their society. The presence of the North in the United States made this impossible for white southerners.

But the *similarities* between the racist behavior of the white South and South Africa are what struck me deeply. The longer I stayed, the angrier I got. My anger erupted on the second day of our visit. It happened at the University of Potchefstroom while I was talking with an Afrikaner professor of theology who was also a member of the smaller of the Dutch Reformed churches, the Nederduitsch Hervormde Kerk. As I sat there listening to this white Afrikaner theologian present his theological reasons for separate development, I thought about white American theologians who did the same thing in relation to slavery and segregation. I looked at this white man with anger in my eyes and said, "You must think we are stupid, talking like that in our presence."

His face suddenly became whiter with obvious anger. He

turned to our host, ignoring me as one to whom remarks need not be directed, and said, "I demand that Professor Cone apologize for that comment!"

A deep silence engulfed the room. Our host then apologized by saying, "Professor Cone merely meant that he could not understand how you can defend separate development on the basis of the Christian gospel."

But the Afrikaner would not accept that explanation. "I demand an apology or I am leaving," he said, raising the volume of his voice for emphasis.

I sat there knowing that not even the threat of death would ever make me apologize to a white racist. Me apologize to an Afrikaner, after what they have done and are still doing to my people? Oh, no, not a chance! After a few seconds, the Afrikaner left the room swiftly, obviously very upset that a black man had spoken to him as an equal. The others remained and apologized for the behavior of their colleague. But they said nothing while he was present.

2. There are a few white liberals in South Africa, but most are too scared to speak out. They reminded me of the white moderates in the South during the early stages of the civil rights movement. Martin Luther King, Jr., was greatly disappointed by them, because they failed to respond to the demands of the gospel and human decency. Instead, most remained silent. Others attacked him for moving too fast. Some even labeled him an outside agitator, charges to which he responded with his classic "Letter from Birmingham Jail."

Many black South Africans share similar views regarding their liberals. But black nationalists often describe them as their worst enemies, because, while they claim to be for justice, white liberals are unprepared to take the risks necessary for its implementation. Unless a larger number of whites develop the courage to take a more radical stand against apartheid, with words and deeds, a racial war seems unavoidable.

3. There are more leaders of the black resistance against apartheid than just Desmond Tutu and Alan Boesak. Of course Tutu and Boesak play important roles in communicating the meaning of the black struggle to an international public and in providing a theological interpretation of it. But I was greatly impressed by the presence of grassroots leaders who have arisen from the resistance movement itself. They are mostly young peo-

ple between the ages of twelve and eighteen. They are not afraid
of death, and they refuse to listen to their elders who counsel
patience. With stones and clenched fists they confront armed
South African police officers with a determination to assert their
dignity and claim their freedom. As soon as they are killed or
carted off to prison for torture, new ones take their place. The
South African government is determined to break this youthful
spirit of resistance. But it will not succeed, because the flame of
freedom has been lit in the soul of black people, and it cannot be
put out until justice comes to all.

5. The vast majority of whites know very little about blacks,
because there is so little communication between them. Whites
know only what the government and the media tell them. I was
reminded again of many whites in the United States who know so
little about blacks, especially in the South during the civil rights
movement and in the ghettos of the large cities, such as New
York's Harlem. How can we, black and white together, build a
just society if we do not know each other and do not share in the
responsibility of breaking down the walls that separate us? How
can Christians do theology, preach the gospel, and live in faithful
obedience and *not* actively seek to create *one* community defined
by justice and love rather than racism and hate?

Many liberal white South African theologians do theology as if
it has nothing to do with the struggle against apartheid. I found
that very difficult to understand. But I thought again about white
American theologians who ignored racism during most of American
history and still continue the practice today. As blacks were
being enslaved, lynched, and segregated, many white theologians
at America's most prestigious seminaries and universities talked
about theology as if blacks did not exist. Indeed, an American
theologian of note preceded our visit to South Africa with a much
longer stay, and we were told by several black and white South
Africans that he did not even mention apartheid as a theological
problem. That same theologian, along with many others, also
failed to make the black struggle for justice an important theological
issue during the 1960s.

6. Unfortunately, there is a tension between black nationalists
and others in search of a multiracial society. This conflict is symbolized
in the differences between UDF and AZAPO. It is obvious
that the government in particular and whites generally are seeking
to break the black resistance movement by exploiting this

tension in the black community. Again, I was reminded of similar differences between Martin Luther King, Jr., and Malcolm X, the most articulate spokespersons of the integrationist and nationalist perspectives during the 1960s. Whites, including liberals, exploited these differences in philosophy and thus prevented King and Malcolm X from working together. It was a great loss that they had only one brief meeting and no occasion for serious dialogue regarding their views about black liberation. Let us hope that our South African brothers and sisters will profit from our mistakes.

7. My trip to South Africa not only deepened my convictions about liberation being at the center of the gospel. It also left me with much less tolerance for professional theologians and church leaders (white and black) who view the matter otherwise. It is really difficult for me to understand how any Christian can know of human suffering on such a massive scale as it exists in our world today and still claim that the gospel of Jesus has nothing to say about it. The connection between Jesus' suffering and human suffering ought to be obvious to Christians. That is why Gustavo Gutiérrez says that "We must not speak of the death of Jesus until we speak of the the real death of people."

I hope that Christians will follow that advice. For in Jesus' cross and resurrection the reality of death has been encountered and defeated. But since the full manifestation of that victory is still to come, we must bear witness *now* to God's coming liberation by refusing to obey the agents of death. This is the message of hope I heard preached and saw in the lives of South Africa's black Christians.